Praise for *University of Destruction*

"David Wheaton provides a useful guide to young Christians who want to use biblical guidelines to overcome the most negative elements of academia and youth culture."

> —**Michael Medved**, nationally syndicated radio host and author of *Right Turns*

"If Daniel needed to be prepared before embarking on his 'higher education' (Daniel 1), every Christian teenager thinking of 'higher education' also needs preparation. Mr. Wheaton covers nearly every area one must ponder and understand before such embarkment. Highly recommended. . . ."

> —**David A. Noebel**, president of Summit Ministries

"David Wheaton's book exposes an important problem for Christian students and their parents to consider when shopping for college: Should they follow the crowd and send their child off to a secular university where the predominate worldview is incompatible and hostile toward the Christian faith, or should they send them to a church-related college where faculty may cause them to question the essentials of the faith? Wheaton's suggestion to be prepared for the mental and emotional struggle that college students will encounter in this battle for the Christian worldview is the best option. I would recommend teens and their parents read this book before becoming enamored with the secular universities of this country that do not respect the Christian beliefs and lifestyle. And then I would recommend they consider a Christ-centered college where faculty and staff integrate the Christian faith into all areas of academic and residential life, because it is there that the faith is nourished and grows."

> —**Gary L. Railsback, Ph.D.**, Associate Professor of Education, George Fox University

DAVID WHEATON

UNIVERSITY *of* DESTRUCTION

YOUR GAME PLAN FOR
SPIRITUAL VICTORY
ON CAMPUS

BETHANYHOUSE
MINNEAPOLIS, MINNESOTA

© 2005 David Wheaton

Published by Bethany House Publishers
11400 Hampshire Avenue South
Bloomington, Minnesota 55438
www.bethanyhouse.com

Bethany House Publishers is a division of
Baker Publishing Group, Grand Rapids, Michigan

Printed in the United States of America

Library of Congress Cataloging-in-Publication Data

Wheaton, David.
     University of destruction : your game plan for spiritual victory on campus / by David Wheaton
        p. cm.
     Summary: "With a conversational style, author David Wheaton explores the three pillars of peril—sex, drugs and rebellion—most often encountered by college students. He then offers students advice on developing a game plan to avoid the spiritual pitfalls" —Provided by publisher.
     ISBN 0-7642-0053-4(pbk.)
     1. College students—Religious life. 2. Sex—Religious aspects—Christianity. 3. Drugs—Religious aspects—Christianity. 4. Conflict of generations. I. Title.
BV4531.3.W47   2005
248.'346—dc22   2005004802

Unless otherwise indicated, Scripture quotations are from the Holy Bible, King James Version.

Scripture quotations identified NLT are from the *Holy Bible*, New Living Translation, copyright © 1996, 2004, 2007 by Tyndale House Foundation. Used by permission of Tyndale House Publishers, Inc., Carol Stream, Illinois 60188. All rights reserved.

All italics in Scripture, added for emphasis, are the author's.

Cover design by Greg Jackson
Interior design by Eric Walljasper

15   16   17   18   19   20   21   18   17   16   15   14   13   12

This book is dedicated to
that *one* young man or young woman
who reads this, heeds this,
. . . and overcomes!

*For whatever is born of God overcomes the world.
And this is the victory that has overcome the world—our
faith. Who is he who overcomes the world, but he who
believes that Jesus is the Son of God?* 1 JOHN 5:4–5

DAVID WHEATON is the host of *The Christian Worldview*, a Minneapolis-based radio program that offers a biblical perspective on current events, culture, and faith. He is also an inspirational speaker and contributing columnist for the *Minneapolis Star Tribune*. Formerly, David was one of the top professional tennis players in the world, attaining a world ranking of number 12, winning the Grand Slam Cup, reaching the semifinals of Wimbledon, representing the United States in Davis Cup competition, and scoring victories over such players as Andre Agassi, Jimmy Connors, Ivan Lendl, Jim Courier, and Michael Chang. In 2004, David won the Wimbledon Over-35 Doubles Championship.

Get connected at *www.davidwheaton.com*!

- Download a chapter-by-chapter study guide
- E-mail the author, post your feedback, and connect with others who have read *University of Destruction*

    . . . and more!

CONTENTS

INTRODUCTION
SUCCESS, SURFING, AND STANFORD

Stanford? Not a problem.

The week before entering my freshman year at Stanford University, I was riding a major wave . . . in more ways than one. I spent the week surfing Pacific rollers in Malibu, California, while visiting my brother, who was toiling away at Pepperdine Law School.

Sitting on my surfboard waiting for the next set of waves to appear, my thoughts drifted back over the previous months—the best summer of my life. In June I had graduated valedictorian of my high school class, and now in September I had just won the U.S. Open Junior Tennis Championships in New York, confirming my place as the top-ranked junior player in America.

I was number one on the court and in the classroom.

How appropriate that in just a few days I would travel up the coast of California to attend the top-rated academic and tennis university in the land . . . on a full scholarship, no less.

While I was riding a perfect wave that golden summer, do you think I was concerned about the next stage of my life in college? Guess again.

Welcome to Stanford

My duffel bags had barely touched the dorm room floor when two tennis teammates-to-be barged through the door with pitchers of beer in hand. It may have been the middle of the afternoon, but the party had already started. Girls and guys roamed the co-ed dorm, checking out their new surroundings. Classes started the next day, and I kid you not, I had neither pen nor paper.

The first assignment in Great Works of Western Culture, a required freshman class, was to read the books of Genesis and Job. "Easy enough," I thought, since I came from a Christian background and was familiar with the Bible. Imagine my disbelief when the professor and other students ridiculed the Bible and mocked God for the "stupid" way He dealt with mankind. I had never heard "God" and "stupid" in the same sentence before! I was so stunned, I didn't know what to say.

The night life was just as shocking. It was as if all moral restraint had been lifted from the campus. Drunkenness and sexual activity were seemingly everywhere. The overall scene brought to mind images of wanton sailors coming ashore at a foreign port of call. Surely this wasn't Stanford—it was Sodom!

Why was I so surprised by my introduction to college? After all, I had heard what college was like. I had already seen and experienced a taste of campus life on college recruiting visits. I was no potted plant—I had been out of my own backyard plenty of times.

But this was different . . . *way* different. I was now living full-time in the midst of a world diametrically opposed to the one I had grown up in—there would be no returning home to Mommy and Daddy every night. I would soon find out that an excellent upbringing coupled with academic and athletic success was no match for the maelstrom called college. The waters were baited, the sharks were circling . . . spiritual shipwreck loomed.

>—•—<

There is one word that perfectly describes my upbringing: *idyllic*. In my memory it was as near to perfect as it could be.

Just west of Minneapolis, Minnesota, my parents' home was perched overlooking Lake Minnetonka in a quaint neighborhood called Cottagewood. Whatever the season, life on the lake encompassed our existence. Swimming and sailing in the summer were followed by ice-skating and cross-country skiing in the winter. Living on the lake was so special to us that my mother would let me stay home from elementary school in early December to skate on the newly frozen black sheet of ice.

Life *off* the lake was storybook too. There was the annual Independence Day parade when all the kids would march around the neighborhood in their patriotic attire. There were the two public tennis courts just down the street from our house where I, at age four, was tossed my first tennis balls by my mother. And there was the outdoor hockey rink across the bay at the local town hall, where my mother would send my brothers and me, saying, "Don't come back till dark."

More than just a lake and a neighborhood, though, what made my childhood especially idyllic was the closeness of our family.

Before I came along, the Wheaton family of five was seemingly complete with my sister, Marnie, followed by my two brothers, Mark and John. But then there were six! My arrival almost nine years after my brother could have generated sibling resentment or apathy toward me. Instead, nonstop affection and attention flowed my way. (Being the youngest can have its advantages, you know.)

My parents set the tone for our family. My father is an even-keeled and kind-hearted man who diligently provided for our middle-class family by working as a mechanical engineer for an air pollution control company near Minneapolis. My mother, dynamic and driven with a keen sense of discernment about people and life, would have been well-suited for a business career but chose to be a homemaker instead. They grew up in the same area, married young, and worked hard to raise a family. This was traditional American stuff.

Most important, my parents based their lives, marriage, and child-rearing on the Christian values found in the Bible, which were not only taught to us, but lived out by them. They were the same people in the home as out of it. We attended church on Sundays and read the Bible together after dinner.

Problems? Arguments? Conflicts? I recall very few.

So it was tennis in the summer and hockey in the winter, with a secure home life wrapped all around me. I entered my teens happy, outgoing, well-adjusted, and successful—academically and athletically. I even played a little piano. My parents (and my brothers and sister, for that matter) had done everything to raise me the right way. By all accounts, I was a good Christian boy.

And then life happened. *Idyllic* rammed into *reality*.

Entering junior high, I encountered a different road being traveled by my teenaged peers than the path my parents were bringing me along back home. Issues like dating, sex, alcohol, drugs, and general rebellion against parents and teachers were at the forefront of their conversation and conduct. It was a conflicting message to me, for sure, but at the same time, this different way also held its allure.

Some would pass it off as growing up, reaching puberty, or meeting the real world, but whatever it was, an almost indiscernible change of course began in my life as I gradually partook in some of the things mentioned. This deviation in junior high proved to be the source, and then high school the staging ground, for my future trouble in college. But I digress. . . .

The Move

Shortly after I won the Minnesota state high school tennis title as a ninth grader at Minnetonka High School, my parents and I moved to Bradenton, Florida, so that I could train at the famed Nick Bollettieri Tennis Academy.

With my dad now working from home as a consulting engineer and my older siblings embarking on their own careers, my parents had the flexibility to uproot themselves from Minnesota and move to Florida.

My tennis improved dramatically during my junior and senior years of high school in Florida as I trained every day after school with future tennis greats like Andre Agassi and Jim Courier. Before long I rocketed to the top of the junior tennis world—elite universities were recruiting, sports agents were visiting, the professional tennis tour was beckoning. Life was as good as it gets for a seventeen-year-old.

The day of my high school graduation brought no valedictory address from me, though, for I was off in Europe with the U.S. National Team playing the Junior French Open and Wimbledon. Returning to America in July, I won a prestigious national junior tournament and then narrowly missed defeating the number one professional player in the world at the time, Ivan Lendl, at a tournament in Washington, D.C. The U.S. Open junior title in New York came a few weeks later, providing a climactic end to an extraordinary summer.

Which brings us back to Malibu. Do you better understand why I wasn't too concerned about the next stage of my life in college at Stanford? As a matter of fact, I didn't even give it a second thought. An idyllic upbringing coupled with remarkable success had bred a bullet-proof confidence within me.

Yet the small cracks that appeared in junior high had continued to expand in high school. It would have been very difficult for even my discerning parents to know that I was susceptible to veering down the wrong path in college. Besides, I was mostly compliant toward them, and in comparison to my peers, I was a pretty good kid.

Being a "good kid" wasn't going to be nearly enough to survive college though. Within a week I had seen enough of college that I called my parents on several occasions telling them I wanted to come home. In an odd moment of clarity, something inside me warned that campus life was going to have a very negative effect on me. My parents listened but wanted me to stay. So I did.

Just two months later the roles reversed. After a campus visit by my parents, they started to see college for what it was and asked me if I would consider dropping out in order to join the professional tennis tour. I listened, but now I wanted to stay. So I did.

Why my change of heart?

In two months' time I began to like college. I made new friends. I went to football games. I enjoyed the tennis team. I read about my athletic exploits in the Stanford newspaper. I bought a motor scooter. I made my own decisions. I had fun at parties. And, oh yeah, I met a cute blond girl.

In short, I adapted to college life. My (paltry) desire to adhere to the Christian values with which I had been raised was overwhelmed by the temptations and pleasures of college life. Drinking at parties didn't seem like such a big deal. The anti-Christian philosophies of my professors didn't bother me as much. And late nights with my girlfriend certainly didn't make me want to leave college now.

Details of my decline in college could be inserted here, but they would only serve to give you a point of reference for your own life ("I would *never* do that!" or "That's *all* he did?"). I am definitely not the standard.

It is enough to say I was an eighteen-year-old off at university . . . the *University of Destruction.*

1. READY? SET? *TRANSITION!*

So will it be tremendous or traumatic . . . your transition to college, that is?

My story notwithstanding, your transition from high school to college has the potential to be positively *tremendous*. If you're prepared, you should be eagerly anticipating it. What an opportunity to gain an education, grow into adulthood, and get ready for your future.

And let's not forget the fun! If you make the right choices, you will have the time of your life in college. What an opportunity to make lifelong friends, create fond memories, and experience a new world.

Going to college—what a potentially tremendous transition for you . . . if you're prepared, and if you make the right choices.

But, *whoops*! The transition can turn *traumatic* in a hurry. You just read my story; you probably have heard many others like it.

Sure, the particulars of any given version are different, but the scenario is exactly the same: Christian boy or girl goes to college and falls away from his or her faith. *Potentially tremendous* turns into *devastatingly traumatic.*

The actual statistic is staggering: *As many as 50 percent of Christian students say they have lost their faith after four years in college.* (See appendix.)

Did you get that? Fifty percent! One out of two! Fifty out of a hundred! Five hundred out of a thousand! That's a lot.

I'm actually not surprised. From what I continually see and hear as a Christian speaker and radio talk show host, I certainly wasn't the only one to suffer spiritual shipwreck in college. It seems like the majority of faith stories from a twenty- or thirty-something details a story of decline in college . . . *even at religious colleges.*

The question is, why? Why is college such a minefield for Christian students?

The answer is actually quite simple: *The majority of Christian teens are spiritually unprepared for the most challenging transition they will ever make in life.*

Transition Defined

The verb *transition* means "to change from one place or state of existence to another." For most of you, that is exactly what will happen when you go to college—you will transition from life at home to life on campus. More than just a change of place, though, your *stage of life* is also in the process of changing from boy to man or girl to woman.

It is the transitional periods in life that are often the most difficult and perilous. *Familiar* is replaced by *new*—new surroundings, new friendships, new temptations . . . new everything!

I believe going off to college is more challenging than some of the other major transitions in life, like moving cross-country, changing careers, or attending a different high school. It might even be more challenging than getting married or having children! (Not that I would know.)

Your Transition to College

But what about your upcoming or recent transition to college? To varying degrees, you have just spent the first eighteen years of your life in familiar and secure surroundings. You went to school and spent time with friends, were involved in after-school activities like sports, music, or work, and then went home to your family in the evening. Perhaps you went to church on Sunday mornings and to youth group on Wednesday nights.

While you associated with your friends quite a bit, much of your time was spent with people older than you—parents, teachers, coaches, employers, youth leaders. Yeah, you spent a little time with your younger brother or sister too.

More often than not, you had to abide by the rules of your house. Sure, you broke them at times, but there was an abiding presence at home limiting your freedom to do whatever you wanted, whenever you wanted. You had to let Dad or Mom know where you were going and with whom, and what time you would return. If you botched your end of the bargain, there were consequences.

In short, you lived a *real life*. You had a daily routine, associated with people of varying ages, and heeded someone's authority. As a matter of fact, you had it *better* than real life because you weren't fully supporting yourself financially. What a deal!

College is going to be different . . . a lot different. First of all, unlike any other time in your past or future, you will be living and spending almost all your time with people your own age. While this may seem perfectly splendid, this is actually *not* ideal because it often fosters an environment of immaturity.

Spending time with people older than we are tends to mature us. Even spending time with younger people can lead to the development of leadership qualities. But I believe spending the majority of your time with those of similar age results only in stunted maturity. The positive influence that parents, teachers, coaches, or other leaders provide won't occur naturally in college because they are simply not around as much. This lack of authority and the same-age dynamic on campus are just two of the ingredients in the recipe for collegiate disaster.

The difference between home life and campus life doesn't end there. Most aspects of college will be solely up to you: registering for classes and getting to them on time, keeping up with schoolwork, feeding and transporting yourself, managing your finances, choosing new friends, doing laundry, and sleeping enough hours to function.

Congratulations—you are now on your own!

And therein lies the major problem: You—a young adult still in the process of maturing mentally, emotionally, physically, and spiritually—are leaving all that is familiar to you for an extremely different and precarious environment that is going to require critical and mature decision-making skills the moment you step on campus.

The transition to college would be less serious if all that mattered was polishing up your personal discipline and time management skills. In reality there are far more important and difficult issues you will have to face in college, namely the three Pillars of Peril, which I'll explain in chapter three.

Better be prepared, for you are going to be smack-dab in the middle of a *battle for your soul* on campus. What does that mean?

It means that the *broad way that leads to destruction* will be battling and beckoning your soul to stray off the *narrow way that leads to life* (see Matthew 7:13–14). It means that your present, future, and even your afterlife are going to be directly affected by which "way" you choose in college.

An overstatement? Not at all. For example, if you choose to have premarital sex in college, you will be weakening yourself for future sexual immorality and extramarital affairs, which often result in broken marriages and families. If you choose to get drunk or use drugs in college, you will be setting yourself up for all kinds of future trouble and anguish, even bouts of addiction. If you choose to believe the anti-Bible, truth-is-relative philosophies taught by certain professors, you will eventually become unprincipled, unstable, and ungodly in your thoughts and action. If you choose to cheat on exams or schoolwork, you will be desensitizing yourself to future deception in business or taxes.

Yet the opposite is also true. If you navigate the troubled waters of college successfully—if you are true to God and His Word—you will be paving the way to a life of purpose and contentment, a life that honors and glorifies God. There is no greater accomplishment than that.

You might be thinking, "College is my four years to experiment. I'm going to have my fun now and settle down later in life." Don't believe the "later" lie. First, you don't know if there will even be a later—no one knows his or her future. And second, you (and everyone else) are not exempt from the consequences of sin just because you're in college, where "everyone else does it" and then *appears* to carry on with no lasting effects.

Rather, the *later truth* is this: *When you choose the beginning of the way in college, you are determining the end of the way later on.* Realize it or not, you are composing your own destiny by your actions in college. And it all starts with your mind.

Consider this process: *A thought becomes an action. An action becomes a habit. A habit becomes your destiny.* Think about that. Your thoughts, your ideas, your views of the world determine what you do and what you will become. In short, they determine who you are as a person.

The Bible states this important principle in the book of Proverbs: "For as he thinks in his heart, so is he" (Proverbs 23:7a).

There it is—what you "think in your heart" will determine your degree of success—or failure—in college.

>—•—<

Everyone knows the positive results of a *tremendous transition* to college: the opportunity for you to gain an education, to grow in maturity, to get prepared for the future, and to have the time of your life. Wow.

Unfortunately, not everyone fully understands, or cares to understand, the other real possibility—the transition to college can turn *traumatic* in a hurry if you're unprepared and make the wrong choices. Whoa.

The purpose of this book is to help you make a tremendous transition to college, all the while avoiding a traumatic one. It is not written to a boy or a girl, but to the young man or young woman that you now are. It will push and it will prod you. You will not find pie-in-the-sky platitudes, but rather practical and powerful ways to make college a University of Instruction, not a University of Destruction.

Ready? (Are you prepared for college?)

Set? (What are you thinking in your heart?)

Transition! (Tremendously, not traumatically.)

VERY IMPORTANT PRINCIPLE:

Although the transition to college can be difficult and dangerous, how you think on campus will define your destiny.

MESSAGE TO MEMORIZE:

For as he thinks in his heart, so is he. PROVERBS 23:7

2. WHO SHALL OVERCOME?

Before we delve into your college mind-set, let's take a look at a young man who successfully navigated one of history's most difficult transitions. His name was Daniel, and his story offers us the portrait of an Overcomer.

Daniel grew up in a privileged Jewish family in the Middle Eastern town of Jerusalem. He was well-educated, good-looking, and socially adept. He had everything going for him. He even had a strong faith in God.

When Daniel was in his teens, Jerusalem was conquered by the infamous king of the Babylonian empire, Nebuchadnezzar. As part of the takeover, Daniel and some of his teenage friends were taken away from their families and brought hundreds of miles northeast to the great city of Babylon (near modern-day Baghdad, Iraq) to be servants in the king's palace.

Now, becoming a servant in the king's palace entailed more than just putting on an apron and sweeping the floors. To be a servant of the king took three years of intense training. Brainwashing might be a better word for it.

First, Daniel's Jewish name, which meant "God is my judge," was changed to the Babylonian name Belteshazzar, which meant "Bel protect the king." Bel was the name of the supreme idol worshiped in the Babylonian Empire.

Second, Daniel was to be instructed in all the literature and culture of Babylon. This would have been a complete re-education for Daniel because the literature and pagan culture of Babylon were diametrically opposed to his God-centered Jewish upbringing in Jerusalem.

Third, Daniel was offered types of food that were forbidden by Jewish law. Making matters worse, the palace food had been offered to the pagan Babylonian deities as a way of honoring them. The palace menu would have been grossly offensive to Daniel's spiritual beliefs.

In short, the king's goal was to transform a godly Jewish boy into a pagan Babylonian.

For Daniel, this was like going off to college. The transition from home life in Jerusalem to palace life in Babylon was an enormous change. And the stakes were high: The king dealt severely with—even killed—those who didn't conform. Suffice it to say that Daniel's transition to Babylon had serious potential to be his University of Destruction!

Imagine yourself in Daniel's shoes for a moment: As a Christian, how would you handle being taken away from your home in America, sent over to Iraq, given an Islamic name, forced to read the literature of Muhammad, compelled to conform to a vastly different culture, told you had to become a Muslim, and fed, say, wild donkey for dinner? I'm guessing this scenario might present some problems for you . . . or for anyone.

So what happened to Daniel? Did he set aside his faith and become a partaker in Babylonian culture? Did he compromise his beliefs to survive? Did he become another statistic by making a failed traumatic transition?

None of the above. Not only did Daniel survive the transition, he *thrived*. Spending the rest of his life in Babylon, Daniel rose to become an important advisor to several kings and a prophet during two major world empires—Babylonian and Medo-Persian—all without compromising his faith.

The question for Daniel is the same one I posed to you at the end of the last chapter: *What was Daniel's mind-set going into this major transition?*

The book of Daniel in the Bible answers that question: "But Daniel purposed in his heart that he would not defile himself with the portion of the king's delicacies, nor with the wine which he drank . . ." (Daniel 1:8).

"Daniel purposed in his heart." What does that mean? It means that Daniel determined *beforehand* that, while in Babylon, he would not compromise his beliefs. Though not knowing exactly what he was going to face or the consequences for not conforming, Daniel committed beforehand to obey God above all. Daniel made a decision and stuck to it . . . no matter what the cost.

You see, your mind-set going into college is going to determine whether or not you have a chance for victory. If you don't have the right mind-set going in, you'll fall right away and be left digging yourself out of a hole. It's like an athlete who enters competition with the wrong attitude—he or she has very little chance of winning.

Conversely, if you do have the right mind-set going into college, you will start off on the correct path and be primed for victory over the Pillars of Peril.

THREE TYPES OF THINKERS

So let's find out what's on your mind. Are you an Overcomer, a Compromiser, or a Pretender?

Every college-bound young person who professes to be a Christian falls into one of these three categories. Let's get an overview of each one and then hear from them individually.

The Overcomer

The Overcomer has a good idea of the obstacles he will face on campus and has decided beforehand to not compromise his Christian beliefs. As a matter of fact, the Overcomer will use the resources of the Bible to overcome the obstacles in college. The Overcomer has learned how to stand alone and, when necessary, to say to others and himself that big little word—*no*.

The Overcomer may have grown up in a Christian or non-Christian home, but either way, he has made his own personal decision to follow Christ after realizing his sinfulness and need for a Savior and Lord. As a result of that decision, he now has the unique potential and power to be victorious in college through his faith in Christ. While the Overcomer is not perfect, he will not only survive the transition to college but actually thrive. Daniel is the example of an Overcomer.

Now for the interview. "Overcomer, what are your thoughts on these fundamental issues?"

- *College:* "I am going to enjoy and take full advantage of my collegiate experience within the biblical boundaries God has set for my own good and protection."
- *God:* "It is more important for me to please God than to please myself or my peers."
- *The Bible:* "I believe the Bible is inspired by God and is my resource for anything I will face in college."
- *Sin:* "The temporary pleasures of sin are not worth the enduring consequences."
- *Sex:* "God designed sex as a gift for marriage, so I will wait until then."
- *Alcohol:* "Drinking alcohol only leads to further trouble, so I'll avoid it."
- *Humanism:* "To offset this brainwash of professors, I will wash my mind daily with the Word of God."
- *Friends:* "I will spend time with like-minded friends and limit my interaction with those who would pull me in the wrong direction."

The Compromiser

The Compromiser (also known as the Fence Rider) is caught between two minds entering college: She wants to do the right thing, but she doesn't want to miss out on all the "fun" either. (Her definition of fun often involves some type of sin.) She wants to have the best of both worlds and, to do so, becomes skilled at rationalizing.

The Compromiser will often tell you she became a Christian as a young child. If a Compromiser has Christian parents, she grew up thinking they were a little too strict and secretly desired to do the things her friends were doing in high school. She is apt to say, "What's wrong with doing that?" as opposed to the Overcomer, who is apt to say, "What's right with doing that?"

The Compromiser will have a roller-coaster experience in college and leave worse for the wear. She is what the Bible calls a "double-minded [person], unstable in all her ways" (James 1:8). I was the example of a Compromiser in college.

"Compromiser, what are your thoughts on. . . ?"

- *College:* "College will be lots of fun—I'll try not to go 'over the line' though."
- *God:* (When she's around Christians) "God is, like, really important to me." (When she's around non-Christians) "God doesn't come up very much."
- *The Bible:* "I read the Bible once in a while."
- *Sin:* "Sin is bad stuff everyone does, but God understands and always forgives you."
- *Sex:* (When she is not dating) "I'm waiting for marriage." (When she is dating) "We really love each other and are going to get married someday anyway."
- *Alcohol:* "Most people drink much more than I do."
- *Humanism:* "Isn't all truth God's truth?"
- *Friends:* "My friends mean everything to me, and I have *so* many of them."

The Pretender

The Pretender will "purpose in his heart" before going to college, but he will be purposing to have a *smokin' good time*. He does what feels good at the time and gives little thought to the consequences of his choices.

The Pretender will profess, "I'm a Christian—my parents go to such-and-such a church, and I was baptized and/or confirmed when I was younger." Yet the Pretender's actions and words bear very little resemblance to one who is a follower of God. In college the Pretender will be training himself to stumble through one personal tragedy after another in life.

"Pretender, what are your thoughts on. . . ?"

- *College:* "When I finally get away from home, I'm going to have the time of my life! I'm young only once."
- *God:* "He's the man upstairs."
- *The Bible:* "The preacher-guy at church reads it at Christmas and Easter."

- *Sin:* "Sin is doing something that hurts someone else or not loving yourself enough."
- *Sex:* "If you really love each other."
- *Alcohol:* "I drink a little too much once in a while, but I never drive when I do."
- *Humanism:* "Huh?"
- *Friends:* "We're all heading down to Mexico for spring break. Yeah!"

What are you?

I want you to be brutally honest with yourself right now. Whom do you most resemble? Who is your *current* mind-set most like—the Overcomer, the Compromiser, or the Pretender?

Are you an Overcomer? If so, your college experience will be productive and rewarding, yet not without difficulty. The bad news is that even with the right mind-set, there is no such thing as perpetual cruise control in college—you may have made it through high school morally and spiritually unscathed, but college will be a much different and more difficult testing ground. The good news is that you have all the resources to be victorious. This book will help you keep on track.

Are you a Compromiser? You may have tons of "fun" in college, but you're going to leave with lots of guilt and regret because you knew better. The bad news for you is if you keep riding that fence, you may fall off and fall further into sin—there is always a lower level. But the good news is you can become an Overcomer the moment you decide you've had enough of your double-mindedness. This book will help you choose the right track and stay there.

Are you a Pretender? God help you. You will definitely have your fun in college, but you will have corrupted your soul in the process. The sad news for you is that you may not care. But the good news is you can instantly become an Overcomer and turn your life in a whole new direction. This book will help you change tracks.

⟩—•—⟨

Let me close this chapter with a word of hope and encouragement. Right now you may be discouraged about being a Compromiser or Pretender. You may be disappointed that you already veered off course in high school and are distressed that things will only get worse in college.

You may be depressed that you can't seem to reform yourself from recurring sin, or you may be in denial that you're a sinner at all. Or you may be distracted by all you have going on and don't want to think about all this. You may even be disillusioned with God and Christianity. There is no need to despair.

If you forget everything else, remember this: *God is the Master of changing lives.*

From discouragement, disappointment, distress, depression, denial, distraction, and disillusionment, God is able to bring hope, contentment, purpose, love, joy, and holiness. No matter how far you have already fallen, He is ever willing to rescue you from your sin, give you an abundant and victorious life on earth, and reward you with eternal life in heaven! If you search far and wide, you will find no better offer . . . and no better solution.

College is like a multi-year marathon. Just as long-distance runners closely monitor their conditioning levels in the weeks before competition so they can make adjustments in their training to be perfectly prepared, so you too have done precisely the same thing in this chapter—you have gauged your current condition so you know if adjustments need to be made before heading into the "big race" on campus.

What's more, in the next two chapters, you'll get a *preview* of the course obstacles (the three Pillars of Peril) and learn what *adjustments* you need to make to overcome them.

For now, would you, like Daniel, purpose in your heart to be an Overcomer?

VERY IMPORTANT PRINCIPLE:

Purposing in your heart to be an Overcomer in college is the first step toward being one.

MESSAGE TO MEMORIZE:

To him who overcomes I will grant to sit with Me on My throne, as I also overcame and sat down with My Father on His throne. REVELATION 3:21

3. MEET THE PILLARS OF PERIL

There is nothing new under the sun. Ecclesiastes 1:9

King Solomon wrote this proverb thousands of years ago, yet it is still true today. Oh, sure, we have airplanes and computers and snowboards now, but new *things* are not what Solomon was referring to.

Solomon was describing the repetitions of life—how the sun rises and sets, how people toil in their work, how desiring fame and fortune is vanity. It can be summed up like this—you're born, you learn, you work, you eat, you sleep, you live, you die. No one is excluded; we all tread a remarkably similar road.

There is nothing new under the sun—including sin and temptation.

Sin can simply be defined as going your own way in opposition to God's way. As the Creator, Sustainer, and Judge of mankind, God has clearly stated His way in the Bible. The Ten Commandments were continually broken way back then; the *same* Ten Commandments are continually broken now. Sin has been, is, and always will be *the* problem in the world. There is no new sin under the sun.

There aren't any new temptations under the sun either. But this is actually a good thing because every temptation you will face in life has previously been encountered—*and overcome*—by someone, somewhere, sometime. College is no exception—there are no new sinful temptations under the *campus sun*. In each succeeding generation, they just come wrapped in different packages.

So take heart. You won't be facing anything previously unknown in college. The Bible says, "No temptation has overtaken you except such as is common to man" (1 Corinthians 10:13). That was written almost two thousand years ago, and it still applies today.

Where does temptation come from, anyway? The Tempter, of course. You know him as Satan or the devil, and he plays off our inborn sinful tendencies. Satan and his minions have used the same lures to bait people into the trap of sin, generation after generation after generation. Why? Because they *work* for the vast majority of mankind!

But in reality, Satan is just a three-trick pony. All the different temptations you will face in college—and there are many—can be grouped into just three basic categories.

THE PILLARS OF PROMISE OR THE PILLARS OF PERIL?

Have you ever noticed that at many universities and colleges the most prominent building on campus is characterized by several large pillars? Pillars have come to be universally recognized not just as a symbol for the U.S. Supreme Court building but as a symbol of higher education. These massive pillars represent strength, support, and longevity. For college students these pillars promise a better future through education, maturation, and preparation.

At a University of Instruction a student gains an education in various academic fields, grows in maturity from boy to man or from girl to woman, and gets prepared for a career and life as an adult. Fundamentally, these are the three Pillars of Promise that college offers.

Unfortunately, though, the collegiate Pillars of Promise are often perverted and replaced by something completely different. Instead of achieving the promise of a better future as a result of gaining an education, growing in maturation, and getting career preparation, students get distracted and sidetracked by three other pillars that also represent college life but result in a worse future. Choosing and succumbing to these pillars causes a University of Instruction to turn into a University of Destruction.

What are these pillars? Not the Pillars of Promise, they are the *Pillars of Peril*.

The Pillars of Peril are summed up in a very familiar triad: *Sex, Drugs,* and *Rock 'n' Roll*. Every sinful temptation you will ever face in college falls into one of these three categories. Let's find out how.

Sex

The first Pillar of Peril is *Sex*. Sexual sin comes in many varieties—premarital sex, lust, pornography (Internet, movies, magazines), oral sex, homosexuality, adultery, masturbation, strip clubs, sensual dancing and dress, lewd jokes, rape, orgies, fantasies, sexual harassment, incest, bigamy, bestiality, and sexual content in movies, commercials, and television. Did I miss any?

All of these are just different forms of sexual sin. They are perversions of God's design for sex.

If the Tempter can't get you with one of them, he'll try another.

Drugs and Alcohol

The second Pillar of Peril is *Drugs and Alcohol*. The use of drugs and alcohol causes the mind and spirit to be altered. And there are many different ways for this to be accomplished—beer, wine, hard liquor, marijuana, heroin, cocaine, crack, pills, methamphetamine, ecstasy, pain or sleeping medications, GHB (a date rape drug), and even glue sniffing. Once again, there are many different options, but they all fall under the same category and do the same thing—they alter your mental and spiritual state.

If the Tempter can't get you with one of them, he'll try another.

Rock 'n' Roll

The third Pillar of Peril is "*Rock 'n' Roll*." Notice the quotation marks—I'm not speaking musically here, but rather about what rock 'n' roll has historically represented—*rebellion against authority (especially God's)* and *rejection of the Bible*. Whenever God's authority is rejected, even slightly, man and his own flawed reasoning reign—this is what is known as humanism. The third Pillar of Peril would more accurately be named humanism, which is the direct result of rebellion 'n' rejection of God and His Word.

This pillar has a broad reach because it encapsulates every type of thought and action that *rebels* against God and *rejects* the Bible. It could be one of the many godless, man-centered philosophies promoted by teachers at secular (non-religious) colleges such as post-modernism, hedonism, evolution, atheism, or nihilism. This is secular humanism.

Or it could be any of the many man-devised biblical errors that you will encounter at a liberal Christian college, such as: The Bible is not the sole basis for truth and has many inaccuracies and discrepancies; Jesus is not the sinless Son of God and is not the only way to eternal life in heaven; and all religions—Christianity, Islam, Buddhism, New Age, Wicca, etc.—are equal. This is religious humanism.

In short, the R 'n' R pillar is a battle for your mind, a battle for your worldview. It includes every temptation that says, "God may say one thing in the Bible, but He's not my authority, and I'm going to believe and do what I want." When you think of the third pillar, think of the inevitable result of rebellion and rejection of God and the Bible— humanism.

And once again, if the Tempter can't get you with one of them, he'll try another—or even more confusing for you, he'll try to get you side-tracked by several of these erroneous philosophies.

Let's talk fundamentals for a moment. The Pillars of Peril—also known as sin—have been man's downfall ever since Satan first intro-duced them to the first humans, Adam and Eve.

Satan himself was the first "rock 'n' roller," the first one to rebel against God and reject His Word. He then successfully enticed Adam and Eve to do the same in the Garden of Eden, thereby consigning the human race to sin.

It really is a battle between obedience and rebellion. God said the following to Cain, Adam and Eve's son (and the first murderer): "If you do well, will you not be accepted? And if you do not do well, sin lies [crouches] at the door. And its desire is for you. . . ." (Genesis 4:7).

What does God mean? He means that if you obey Him, you will do well and be accepted. But if you *rebel* against God and *reject* His Word, sin is crouching at your door, and its desire is to *destroy* you. Think about that: Satan wants to destroy you through tempting you to sin.

Think I'm making that up? Consider this: "Be sober, be vigilant; because your adversary the devil walks about like a roaring lion, seeking whom he may devour. Resist him, steadfast in the faith, knowing that the same sufferings are experienced by your brotherhood in the world" (1 Peter 5:8–9).

If you remember one thing from this chapter, remember this: The Tempter's desire is to lure you into habitual sin so he can destroy your earthly life and, even more important, your afterlife. He's goin' down, and he wants to take you with him. Don't let him do it! Resist him!

> Therefore submit to God. Resist the devil and he will flee from you. James 4:7

When I hear a student glibly say, "I'm gonna sow my wild oats in college," I sadly think of this passage from the Bible:

> Do not be deceived, God is not mocked; for whatever a man sows, that he will also reap. For he who sows to his flesh will of the flesh reap corruption, but he who sows to the Spirit will of the Spirit reap everlasting life. Galatians 6:7–8

You have a choice in college: You can sow a life that pleases your flesh, or you can sow a life that pleases God. It is completely up to you.

Warning! The three Pillars of Peril pose extreme danger to your soul. Those who wrongly and foolishly minimize their danger are denying the reality that sin stings, enslaves, and spiritually kills.

In college your reality is that these three Pillars *are* perilous and that you must be an Overcomer to conquer them. You'll learn the first essential step next.

VERY IMPORTANT PRINCIPLE:

The Pillars of Peril are tempting and dangerous, but they are nothing new under the sun.

MESSAGE TO MEMORIZE:

Be sober, be vigilant; because your adversary the devil walks about like a roaring lion, seeking whom he may devour. Resist him, steadfast in the faith, knowing that the same sufferings are experienced by your brotherhood in the world. 1 PETER 5:8–9

4. PROFESSORS V. POSSESSORS

All Possessors are Professors, but only *some* Professors are Possessors. Get it?

Before we break down each Pillar of Peril and develop your game plan for victory, we need to discuss the ultra-important difference between *Professors and Possessors*—and I ain't talkin' about your teachers in college!

Let me explain. No doubt you remember the jaw-dropping statistic earlier in the book: *As many as 50 percent of Christian students say they have lost their faith after four years of college.* You, like me, probably wondered, how can this be?

Well, here is the answer: 100 percent of these incoming students were *Professors*, but only 50 percent were actual *Possessors*. Still confused?

To *profess* simply means to make a claim about something. Anyone can make a claim about anything—including their Christian faith. But whether their profession or claim is actually true is a completely different matter.

The Professor

For example, if Fred professes to be a concert pianist, does that necessarily make him one? Of course not! Even if Fred walks around with music books under his arm, talks about the finer points of Beethoven's music, and plays a few songs for his college dorm mates, this certainly doesn't make him a concert pianist, does it? Far from it.

Fred, in reality an amateur pianist, is not just deceiving others, he is deceiving himself too. He may think, "I'm a concert pianist—I know a lot about piano and did play a *concert of sorts* for my dorm mates."

Nevertheless, even if Fred (and everyone else) believes that he's a concert pianist, it certainly doesn't make it so. The reality is that if Fred played under the pressure of a real concert in a large auditorium in front of thousands of people, he would be discovered to be a fraud in about one minute. He doesn't *possess* the qualities of a concert pianist.

Fred's claim would be a faulty *profession*. Despite his personal belief, Fred is nothing more than a novice who can play a few songs on the piano. And perhaps worse than his lack of skill, Fred has deluded himself and others along the way.

The Possessor

Now meet another Professor—Tom. Tom, too, professes to be a concert pianist—he walks around with music books under his arm, talks about the finer points of Beethoven, and plays a few tunes for his college dorm mates once in a while.

But when Tom gets on the stage of a large auditorium in front of thousands of people, he actually can play the piano to the level of a concert pianist. Under pressure, Tom is able to perform because he truly has the genuine characteristics of a concert pianist.

So what is the difference between Fred and Tom? Fred is merely a Professor, while Tom is a Possessor. Tom actually *possesses* the qualities that define a concert pianist, while Fred does not.

I'm sure you see where I am going with this analogy. The point is that anyone can profess to be a Christian, but only those Professors who actually *possess* a genuine Christian faith have the potential to be victorious in college . . . and in life.

Now, let's clarify the study of incoming college students who claimed to be "born-again" Christians:

- One hundred percent of the students in the study *professed* to have a Christian faith.
- The 50 percent who said they *lost their faith* after four years in col-

lege were either severely backslidden due to sin or doubt at the time of the survey, or they didn't actually possess a genuine saving faith to begin with—the testing fire of college proved them to be mere Professors, not Possessors.

Either way, their condition (backslidden) or their position (Professor only) needs to change to be an Overcomer. Perhaps the term "lose their faith" needs to change too—I strongly believe the Bible teaches that Possessors can't, won't, and don't "lose their faith." The gift of faith they have received from God endures—it cannot be lost, stolen, or taken away. At the time of salvation, true believers are given the indwelling Holy Spirit as a seal from God—the Spirit comes in to stay . . . forever. Jesus affirmed this when He said:

> And I will pray the Father, and He will give you another Helper, *that He may abide with you forever*—the Spirit of truth, whom the world cannot receive, because it neither sees Him nor knows Him; but you know Him, for He dwells with you and *will be in you.* John 14:16–17
>
> My sheep hear My voice, and I know them, and they follow Me. And I give them eternal life, and they shall never perish; neither shall anyone snatch them out of My hand. My Father, who has given them to Me, is greater than all; and no one is able to snatch them out of My Father's hand. John 10:27–29

The important point is that there is a world of difference between a Professor and a Possessor. Professors "lose their faith" in college because they never really had it to begin with. Possessors never lose their faith because God has promised to sustain the faith He has given to them. Sure, Possessors may fall or stray off course at times, but God is there to help them get back on track.

The following is the most important sentence in this book: **You must be a Possessor to be an Overcomer in college.** The one prerequisite for victory on campus is to be a Possessor of a genuine saving faith in Jesus Christ.

Self-Test: Professor or Possessor?

Before you face the three Pillars of Peril on campus, you first absolutely need to know—are you a Professor or a Possessor?

There is only one way to find out: Examine yourself. The Bible says that all professing Christians should "examine yourselves as to whether you are in the faith. Test yourselves" (2 Corinthians 13:5a).

So test yourself; see whether you are actually "in the faith." Being "in the faith" means you are more than just a Professor; you are a Possessor too.

And testing yourself does not mean testing the faith or religious traditions of your parents or family. This is a personal and individual examination of *you*. As the saying goes, "God doesn't have *grandchildren;* He only has *children*."

How do you test yourself? Read the following statements and check the boxes that describe your personal beliefs about your faith.

☐ I agree that I have broken many of God's laws (for example, the Ten Commandments), which makes me a sinner, and thus, alienated from God.

> For all have sinned and fall short of the glory of God. Romans 3:23

☐ I realize that God is so offended by my sin that He would be fully justified in making me pay the most severe penalty for it—eternity in hell.

> For the wages of sin is death. Romans 6:23
>
> And I saw the dead, small and great, standing before God, and books were opened. And another book was opened, which is the Book of Life. And the dead were judged according to their works, by the things which were written in the books. . . . And anyone not found written in the Book of Life was cast into the lake of fire. Revelation 20:12, 15

☐ I understand that God, despite my sin, loved me so much that He sent to earth His own sinless Son, Jesus Christ, to die on the cross in my place for my sin.

> For God so loved the world [you] that He gave His only begotten Son, that whoever believes in Him should not perish but have everlasting life. John 3:16

☐ I trust that Jesus' perfect sacrifice of himself on the cross satisfied God's wrath for my sin, thus saving me from going to hell and granting me eternity in heaven instead.

> For [God] made [Jesus] who knew no sin to be sin for us, that we

might become the righteousness of God in Him. 2 Corinthians 5:21

☐ I believe there is no other way to God and eternal life in heaven apart from a personal faith in Jesus Christ.

> Jesus said . . . "I am the way, the truth, and the life. No one comes to the Father except through Me." John 14:6

☐ I commit my life to following and obeying my Savior and Lord, Jesus Christ.

> He who has My commandments and keeps them, it is he who loves Me. John 14:21a

☐ I believe that every word in the Bible is inspired by God and is absolute truth.

> All Scripture is given by inspiration of God. 2 Timothy 3:16a
> Sanctify them by Your truth. Your word is truth. John 17:17

☐ I spend time with God regularly through reading the Bible and praying, so I can become more like Jesus Christ.

> As newborn babes, desire the pure milk of the word, that you may grow thereby, if indeed you have tasted that the Lord is gracious. 1 Peter 2:2–3
> For whom [God] foreknew [you], He also predestined to be conformed to the image of His Son, that He might be the firstborn among many brethren. Romans 8:29

☐ I fellowship with other Christians and share my faith with non-Christians at opportune times.

> But if we walk in the light as He is in the light, we have fellowship with one another. 1 John 1:7a
> Always be ready to give a defense to everyone who asks you a reason for the hope that is in you. 1 Peter 3:15b

☐ I overcome the trials and temptations of life with the supernatural resources God provides, but when I do fall short, I immediately confess my sin.

> I have been crucified with Christ; it is no longer I who live, but Christ lives in me; and the life which I now live in the flesh I live by faith in the Son of God, who loved me and gave himself for me. Galatians 2:20
> If we confess our sins, He is faithful and just to forgive us our sins and to cleanse us from all unrighteousness. 1 John 1:9

So what do you think? Did you check all the boxes? The above statements of faith describe the transformation of a heart from unbeliever to believer, from Professor to Possessor.

If you're still not sure whether you are "in the faith," perhaps comparing two lists from the book of Galatians will help you come to a conclusion.

Is your life characterized by any of these things? Do you *practice* one or more of the following on a regular basis?

> Now the works of the flesh are evident, which are: adultery, fornication, uncleanness, lewdness, idolatry, sorcery, hatred, contentions, jealousies, outbursts of wrath, selfish ambitions, dissensions, heresies, envy, murders, drunkenness, revelries, and the like; of which I tell you beforehand, just as I also told you in time past, that those who *practice* such things will not inherit the kingdom of God. Galatians 5:19–21

Or is your life characterized by this next list?

> But the fruit of the Spirit is love, joy, peace, patience, kindness, goodness, faithfulness, gentleness, self-control. Galatians 5:22

Just like a concert pianist is characterized by knowledge of the piano, daily practice, and performance under pressure, so a Possessor is characterized by fellowship with God, living righteously, and persevering under the pressures of life. Yes, Possessors do sin, but habitual sin is not the *recurring pattern* of their lives. They don't *practice* sin like unbelievers. And when they do sin, they confess it to God and turn away from it.

Bad News . . . Good News

If your life does not fit the profile of a Possessor, but rather is characterized by recurring sin, I have some bad news—you are a Professor only.

But I also have some incredibly good news! Jesus came to earth to offer the following bad news/good news message of hope:

> Repent, and believe in the gospel. Mark 1:15b

The bad news comes first—you need to repent because your sin has alienated you from God. "Repent" means you have a change of mind about your sin; it means you realize your sin has offended God and you need His help to turn away from it.

The good news comes next—*gospel* literally means "good news." The gospel or good news is that Jesus came to die for your sin so that your sin debt to God can be forgiven and you can spend eternity with Him in heaven. There is no better news than that!

So there it is—amazingly simple but incredibly profound. You can become a Possessor by

- agreeing with God that you are a sinner
- repenting of your sin (turning away from it)
- believing in Jesus Christ as your Savior from sin and then following Him as the Lord of your life

If becoming a Possessor—a true believer—is the desire of your heart, why don't you settle this issue right now and become a possessor of a genuine saving faith in Jesus Christ. You can do it by praying something like this:

Heavenly Father, I am deeply sorry that I have sinned against you. I want to turn away from all my sin and need your help to chart a new course. I believe that your Son, Jesus, came to earth to die on the cross for my sin so that I may receive forgiveness and eternal life in heaven. I believe that Jesus is my Savior from sin, and I also commit to follow Him for as long as I live on this earth. I gratefully receive your promise of the indwelling Holy Spirit right now. Father, thank you for loving me and giving me this precious gift of salvation. Amen.

If this is your commitment of faith, congratulations! You have made *the most important* decision anyone can ever make in life—you have become a Possessor! You now possess a genuine saving faith and the indwelling Holy Spirit. You were once born physically; now you have been born spiritually—"born again" (1 John 1:1–8). Your own spirit has been made alive—you now have a spiritual birthdate! You may have a very emotional experience, or you may not. More important than any feeling is your faith commitment to Jesus Christ as your Savior and Lord. The angels in heaven are rejoicing over you right now!

> Likewise, I say to you, there is joy in the presence of the angels of God over one sinner who repents. Luke 15:10

You are on your way toward being an Overcomer!

A Word About Works

Contrary to every religion in the world besides genuine biblical Christianity, a saving faith in Jesus Christ does not stem from "being religious"—doing good works in the attempt to please or justify yourself to God.

God is definitely not impressed, and you are certainly not saved by being born into a Christian family, infant baptism, being confirmed, church or youth group attendance, giving to charity, or believing you're a good person. He is not even impressed with a childhood or teenage profession of faith if it didn't involve genuine repentance and continuing trust in Jesus Christ.

Not only are these supposed "good works" not good and not enough, they're considered *filthy* to God:

> But we are all like an unclean thing, and all *our righteousnesses* are like filthy rags. Isaiah 64:6a

You see, God is *perfectly holy*, and He can let only perfect people abide with Him in heaven. Trying to do good works—like going to church, praying a lot, being nice to people, giving money to charity—to earn your way to heaven is as futile as attempting to jump across the Grand Canyon—some people may do better and jump farther than others, but every single person will end up in the canyon below.

The *only* way to get to heaven is God's way—faith alone in Christ alone. God even gives you the grace—the power—to have that saving faith. He offers you a gift; you just receive it by faith.

> For by grace you have been saved through faith, and that not of yourselves; it is the gift of God, *not of works*, lest anyone should boast. Ephesians 2:8–9

When you repent of your sin and believe in Jesus Christ as your Savior and your Lord, God transfers the perfect, sinless righteousness of Jesus Christ to you. He no longer sees you as a condemned sinner; He sees you as a perfect saint! You, a Possessor, will still sin on occasion, but God now sees you as sinless because all your past, present, and future sin has been fully paid for and covered by Jesus Christ.

Read again this amazing verse proving this important point:

> For [God] made Him [Jesus] who knew no sin to be sin for us, that we might become the righteousness of God in Him. 2 Corinthians 5:21

So are good deeds bad? Of course not. They should be the natural result of a converted and renewed heart. When they're done with the right motive after you're saved, then the deeds can be, in fact, good. Remember, faith justifies, good deeds exemplify.

Believer Beware!

You have now heard the "gospel" or "good news." Now for a word of caution: Becoming and being a Possessor is not easy. You will have to exit off the main highway onto a much less traveled road. You will be going against the grain of our culture. You will be swimming upstream. You can no longer be on the throne of your life—Jesus Christ must be.

Jesus described becoming and being a Possessor this way:

On *becoming* a Possessor:

> Enter by the narrow gate; for wide is the gate and broad is the way that leads to destruction, and there are many who go in by it. Because narrow is the gate and difficult is the way which leads to life, and there are few who find it. Matthew 7:13–14

On *being* a Possessor:

> If anyone desires to come after Me, let him deny himself, and take up his cross daily, and follow Me. For whoever desires to save his life will lose it, but whoever loses his life for My sake will save it. Luke 9:23–24

A "narrow gate" of entry for a "few" souls. A life of self-denial. Health, wealth, and prosperity not guaranteed. Suffering and persecution, on the other hand, guaranteed.

The immaterial rewards, though, of becoming a Possessor are many and great. First and foremost, you will fulfill the purpose for which you were created—to fellowship with the One who created you. You will have found the key to inner contentment and wisdom. You will spend eternity with God in heaven and avoid being justly sent to hell.

Jesus summarized it perfectly:

> The thief [Satan] does not come except to steal, and to kill, and to destroy. I have come that they may have life, and that they may have it more abundantly. John 10:10

Think of it—Jesus came to earth to save you from being destroyed by Satan by offering you eternal life with Him in heaven. That's an offer you shouldn't refuse.

A Possessor's Secret to Success

Let me close the chapter by telling you an important secret about Professors and Possessors: Possessors have potential, but mere Professors have problems.

Another riddle? No. What I mean is that only Possessors, *real Christians*, have the *potential* to make it through college without losing their faith. You see, Possessors have something in them that no one else has—they have the Holy Spirit of God.

At the moment you pray to God and truly believe in Jesus Christ as your Savior and Lord, God sends His Holy Spirit to indwell you for the *rest* of your life.

Jesus said this to His followers:

> I will pray the Father, and He will give you another Helper, that He may abide with you forever—the Spirit of truth, whom the world cannot receive, because it neither sees Him nor knows Him; but you know Him, for He dwells with you and will be in you. John 14:16–17

You need this "Helper" to get through college . . . to get through life. Without Him, you won't make it.

The Holy Spirit is pure power. Did you know that the same Spirit that raised Jesus Christ from the dead dwells in you if you are a true Christian?

> But if the Spirit of Him who raised Jesus from the dead

dwells in you, He who raised Christ from the dead will also give life to your mortal bodies through His Spirit who dwells in you. Romans 8:11

If the Holy Spirit can raise Jesus from the dead, do you think He can give you the power to overcome the three Pillars of Peril? Of course He can! At your moment of need, He is there to help you be an Overcomer.

Your responsibility is to listen to and obey Him. Here's how He operates:

But the Helper, the Holy Spirit, whom the Father will send in My name, He will teach you all things, and bring to your remembrance all things that I said to you. John 14:26

Love God, Fear God

The indwelling Holy Spirit will teach and remind you of what you read in God's Word. He will help you develop two ultra-important qualities of an Overcomer: a *love* of God and a *fear* of God.

A *love of God* in that your desire to please Him will be much greater than your desire to please yourself when confronted with temptation. And a *fear of God* in that you will want to avoid offending Him and suffering the discipline that comes with sin.

The perfect balance of loving God and fearing God is what motivates, drives, and inspires a Possessor to be an Overcomer. This is so key. All the practical biblical advice coming your way in the ensuing chapters on overcoming the three Pillars of Peril will have little effect unless you have a strong love and fear of God—nothing else will motivate you to get on the right path and stay off the wrong road.

The great news is that the indwelling Spirit will help you grow in your love and fear of the Lord:

The love of God has been poured out in our hearts by the Holy Spirit who was given to us. Romans 5:5
And by the fear of the Lord one departs from evil. Proverbs 16:6b

But the Holy Spirit is a gentleman—He will not force himself on you. He is "available power," which means that you can choose to obey

Him or not. Remember, the Holy Spirit teaches and reminds . . . it's up to you to listen and obey.

This is why mere Professors (i.e., Compromisers and Pretenders) will have problems in college and will fall time after time. They don't have the indwelling power and inner motivation (i.e., a love and fear of the Lord) to be Overcomers. They might score a few victories here and there with their own finite strength, but their overall trend will be to fail. They may say they "lost their faith," but the reality is that they never had a faith to begin with.

Possessors, on the other hand, aren't immune to problems in college and will fall at times, but practicing sin won't characterize their lives, and they will always get back to being Overcomers. They don't lose their faith in college because they can't—what God has given endures to the end!

Did you discover whether you are a Professor or a Possessor? If you are just a Professor, did you decide to become a Possessor? Your decision will make all the difference whether you overcome in college or whether you compromise and stumble your way through.

I hope and pray you made the right choice because when you turn the page, the first Pillar of Peril will be there waiting for you.

VERY IMPORTANT PRINCIPLE:

To survive the Pillars of Peril in college, you must be more than a mere Professor; you must be a Possessor of a true faith in Jesus Christ.

MESSAGE TO MEMORIZE:

Examine yourselves as to whether you are in the faith. Test yourselves. 2 CORINTHIANS 13:5A

PERSONAL COMMITMENT:

I have repented of my sin and believe in Jesus Christ as my Savior and will trust Him as the Lord of my life.

Signature:

Date:

5. THE FIRST PILLAR OF PERIL—SEX

Sex. Sex. Sex. Sex. Sex. Sex is here, sex is there, sex is *everywhere*—especially on college campuses! That is why sex is your first Pillar of Peril.

Whether it's the rampant sexual behavior of students, the "sexual liberation" philosophies of the professors, or the campus-wide, sexually charged environment, sexual immorality permeates life in college. It is impossible to avoid its presence.

Think about the following "recipe": Mix together in co-ed dorms young men and young women with simmering sexual desires, remove parental and church authorities, add teachers who glamorize sexual exploration, throw in generous amounts of alcohol, and now tell me, what do you think will be the result?

Sexual immorality, in all its forms, is not just accepted on college campuses, it is greatly *encouraged*. It is a wonder anyone makes it through college sexually unscathed.

Years ago, author and philosopher Aldous Huxley aptly articulated the collegiate attitude toward sexual promiscuity: "We will not bow to your God because He would interfere with our sexual mores [morals]."

At least he's honest. And exactly right. God's design for sex is the defining line between moral *purity* and moral *perversity*. Since God and the Bible are often discounted and dismissed on college campuses as "outdated" and "repressive," it is not surprising that there is very little interference to sexual sin.

Rather than bowing to God, sexual immorality, at its fundamental level, is about worshiping the body rather than the *Creator* of the body. The apostle Paul could very well have been describing life on today's campuses in this passage from the book of Romans:

> Therefore God also gave them up to uncleanness, in the lusts of their hearts, to dishonor their bodies among themselves, who exchanged the truth of God for the lie, and worshiped and served the [body] rather than the Creator. Romans 1:24–25

This is precisely what happens in college—students are seduced into dishonoring their bodies, and thus, dishonoring God. They worship and serve their physical desires rather than God. Be not mistaken, though, *Christians are not immune.*

Remember the seemingly endless list of all the ways sexual immorality presents itself on campus—premarital sex, lust, pornography (Internet, movies, magazines), oral sex, homosexuality, adultery, masturbation, strip clubs, sensual dancing and dress, lewd jokes, rape, orgies, fantasies, sexual harassment, incest, bigamy, bestiality, and sexual content in movies, commercials, and television? Satan has certainly devised plenty of different baits to lure people into sexual sin.

Good Sex

With all the myriad manifestations of sexual sin, God's design for sex is sometimes lost in the shuffle. Yet He couldn't be more clear about His standard:

> Marriage is honorable among all, and the bed undefiled; but fornicators and adulterers God will judge. Hebrews 13:4

There it is—God designed sex for married couples. Sex is "honorable" within marriage, but God will judge those who have premarital or extramarital sex. God is saying once you're married, sex with your spouse is all yours—for bonding, for procreating, for enjoyment. This is sexual morality as defined by God. This is God's standard.

Bad Sex

Therefore, if sex within the bounds of marriage is moral, right, pure, and downright divine, what does God say about the opposite— sexual immorality?

> For this is the will of God, your sanctification [holiness]: that you should abstain from sexual immorality. 1 Thessalonians 4:3

One thing about God is that He makes this issue very clear. Let's not complicate it. God's will is that all people—unmarried and married—*abstain* from sexual immorality. It can't be stated any more clearly than that.

Sexual immorality is much broader in scope than just the act of sexual intercourse between unmarried people. It includes any deed *and thought* that opposes God's design for sex within marriage.

Mind Sex

Yes, God does not stop with our physical actions as the only types of sexual immorality to be avoided. God's standard is that we do not commit sexual immorality in our minds either. Sexual immorality in our minds is called *lust*. It is the mental craving for sex.

In the gospel of Matthew, Jesus *equates* the literal act of adultery with the lustful thought of it.

> But I say to you that whoever looks at a woman to lust for her has already committed adultery with her in his heart. Matthew 5:28

This changes everything. God not only expects our actions to be pure, but our thoughts to be pure as well. In the eyes of God, lust and immoral sexual acts are one and the same.

Like every other sin, sexual immorality begins in the mind. The course of events is perfectly predictable: Sexual temptation enters the mind through a sight, a sound, a touch, or a thought, and then turns into the sin of lust if not replaced immediately. And then, too often, once lust mushrooms in the mind, it is only a matter of time before it is acted upon physically.

> But each one is tempted when he is drawn away by his own

desires and enticed. Then, when desire has conceived, it gives birth to sin; and sin, when it is full-grown, brings forth death. James 1:14–15

It is *always* the same pattern. *This is why you must fight and win the battle for moral purity in your mind.*

Sweet . . . Bitter

Why is God's design for sex so narrow? The reason is He wants to *save* you—save you *from* hurting yourself physically, emotionally, and spiritually, and save you *for* your future spouse. He knows that sexual immorality ruins lives—children are born out of wedlock, abortions occur, guilt and emotional scars besiege, marriages are lost, diseases are contracted, and rape and incest result. Yet many people (perhaps most) disregard His design.

So with all the negatives from sexual immorality, why would anyone want to get involved in it, even once? That's simple—sex, like many sins, is pleasurable! God designed sex to be pleasurable physically, emotionally, and spiritually . . . yet to be enjoyed *within* marriage. There is pleasure in sin for a season, but that's just the point: it's only for a *season* before the consequences are reaped. Satan will always show you the beautiful, tempting, and pleasurable beginning of sexual immorality, but he will *never show you* the bitter end.

The book of Proverbs uses the following analogy for sexual sin:

> [The world says,] "Stolen water is sweet, and bread eaten in secret is pleasant." Proverbs 9:17
> But in the end [immorality] is bitter as wormwood. Proverbs 5:4

Sexual sin may be "sweet" and "pleasant" in the beginning, but the bitter end is unavoidable.

We're halfway home on this first Pillar of Peril. You now know that college and sexual immorality go together like hand in glove. You know that God has designed sex for marriage. You know sexual immorality includes both deeds *and* thoughts. And you know that sexual immorality will ruin your life. What else do you need to know?

How to be an Overcomer, of course! How to have victory over this

Pillar of Peril. Let's take a look at a young man named Joseph who was victorious.

Joseph the Overcomer

Like you in college and Daniel in Babylon, Joseph faced a difficult transition. Joseph grew up in what is modern-day Israel, but he was sold by his own brothers into slavery in Egypt because they were jealous of Joseph's most-favored status with their father.

So, much like Daniel, Joseph rose from being a slave to being in charge of the house of Potiphar, who was Pharaoh's captain of the guard. Talk about moving up in society! Joseph had great position and responsibility, not to mention prestige.

And then it happened. Potiphar's own wife approached the good-looking young man, Joseph, and said bluntly (and no doubt seductively), "Lie with me." She certainly didn't use much subtlety, but perhaps with her position she didn't have to. Whatever the case, Joseph had two choices: please his master's wife (and his own flesh) or please God.

Which did he choose? You've probably heard this story, but it's interesting to notice Joseph's response to her:

> But he refused and said to his master's wife, "Look, my master does not know what is with me in the house, and he has committed all that he has to my hand. There is no one greater in this house than I, nor has he kept back anything from me but you, because you are his wife. How then can I do this great wickedness, and sin against God?" Genesis 39:8–9

Simply stated, Joseph refused her advance because it was more important to him to please God than to please himself or her—that is what it means to love God first and foremost. One could also say that Joseph's fear of offending God was even greater than his fear of the consequences of adultery (guilt, public shame, perhaps death). Joseph's love and fear of God kept him from sin.

Potiphar's wife didn't give up, though. She wasn't going to take no for an answer. The chase continued.

> So it was, as she spoke to Joseph day by day, that he did not heed her, to lie with her or to be with her. But it happened about this time, when Joseph went into the house to do his work, and

none of the men of the house was inside, that she caught him by his garment, saying, "Lie with me." But he left his garment in her hand, and fled and ran outside. Genesis 39:10–15

Now, there are aggressive women, and there are *aggressive* women! Her day-by-day persistence finally reached a point where she grabbed him by his coat and tried to pull him into bed. This time words weren't going to stop her—Joseph *fled* the scene, leaving his coat in her hands. Joseph was an Overcomer.

King David . . . Overcome!

Let's compare Joseph's response to sexual temptation with another man of great authority, King David—one who is described as "a man after [God's] own heart" (1 Samuel 13:14).

> It happened in the spring of the year, at the time when kings go out to battle, that David sent Joab and his servants with him, and all Israel; and they destroyed the people of Ammon and besieged Rabbah. But David remained at Jerusalem.
>
> Then it happened one evening that David arose from his bed and walked on the roof of the king's house. And from the roof he saw a woman bathing, and the woman was very beautiful to behold.
>
> So David sent and inquired about the woman. And someone said, "Is this not Bathsheba, the daughter of Eliam, the wife of Uriah the Hittite?" Then David sent messengers, and took her; and she came to him, and he lay with her, for she was cleansed from her impurity; and she returned to her house. And the woman conceived; so she sent and told David, and said, "I am with child." 2 Samuel 11:1–5

Did you notice the chain of events? David was shirking his responsibility to lead Israel into battle (v. 1)—he had too much idle time on his hands. David then saw Bathsheba bathing, lusted after her in his mind, had her brought to his palace to have sex, and impregnated her.

A *look* became a *lust* became an *action*. It is always the same pattern.

Predictably, here was the bitter result: David had Bathsheba's husband killed, the illegitimate child ended up dying, and David's kingdom was overthrown by his own son. One sin begets another sin begets another begets severe consequences. Don't be fooled to think there aren't major consequences for sexual sin—even after we repent (as David eventually did—Psalm 51). No one ever gets away with sin.

Unlike Joseph, David decided to please his flesh rather than please God. At that moment he loved himself more than he loved God. He lost sight of his fear of the Lord.

Both of them Possessors, Joseph and David were each presented with sexual temptation: Joseph overcame; David was overcome.

The Plan for Purity

All right, let's get very practical on how you can overcome the first Pillar of Peril in college. The following six steps will help you be an Overcomer, whether you're sexually pure, have already fallen, or keep falling into sexual sin. Here's your plan for purity:

1. Commit to moral purity. Just like Daniel purposed in his heart that he would not defile himself in Babylon, you too need to make a personal commitment to moral purity, both in thought and deed, to have any chance of victory. You won't survive if you just "see how it goes." Write down your commitment and the date you made it. Wear a ring or a bracelet if it will help you remember.

And then take it one step further—tell your parents or your closest friend about your commitment to moral purity and ask him or her to hold you *accountable* on a regular basis. Sexual immorality is almost always done in secret, whether in the privacy of your bedroom or your mind. When you know your dad or mom or friend or youth pastor is going to ask you weekly or monthly if you have maintained moral purity, you will be amazed how this will affect your thoughts and behavior. Remember, though, sexual sin and lying are bedfellows—you must commit to being totally truthful, *no matter what*, to your accountability partner.

Want to *depart* from moral impurity? Love the Lord—please and obey Him rather than your own desires. Fear the Lord—know that the Lord is continually watching and weighing your every thought and action and will hold you accountable for each one. And *fear* your friend—know that your accountability partner will ask you every week or month how you're doing and will even be willing to come and get you out of a tempting situation. Now, that is a powerful triad to help you keep your commitment to moral purity!

I know what some of you are thinking—"I've already fallen" or "I can't break away from sexual immorality." For those of you who have lost your virginity, have recurring lustful thoughts, are dabbling with pornography, are in a cycle of masturbation, or are involved in any other form of sexual immorality, I have very good news for you—it is never too late to make a commitment to moral purity! If you truly are a Possessor, you have all the resources you need to overcome moral impurity. Make your commitment to moral purity today and become accountable to a parent or a friend; the Holy Spirit and God's Word will be there to give you the power for victory.

2. Guard your eyes. A man named Job was described by God as "a blameless and upright man, one who fears God and shuns evil" (Job 1:8). Now, that's a high compliment! This is what Job said about his eyes and lust: "I have made a covenant with my eyes; why then should I look upon a young woman?" (Job 31:1). Job made a contract with his eyes to not lust after women.

When King David looked down from his palace roof and saw Bathsheba bathing, he hadn't sinned . . . yet. *Temptation is not sin,* but temptation will turn into sin very quickly if immediate action is not taken. David sinned when he *"beheld"* or lingered in watching Bathsheba bathe. Instead of averting his eyes, David fueled lustful passion in his mind by continuing to look at her. And you know the rest of the story.

You, like Job, need to make a covenant with your eyes that you will not linger on *anything* that will cause you to lust—a seductively dressed woman in the hallway of your dorm, a shirtless man playing sports, magazine advertisements, an email with sensual images, movies, billboards, TV shows, commercials . . . anything that causes you to lust! Train yourself to avert your eyes immediately. Turn your head, close your eyes, avert your gaze . . . do not let a tempting sight become a sinful thought. Make the Psalmist's commitment your own: "I will set nothing wicked before my eyes" (Psalm 101:3a).

3. Guard your thoughts. Sometimes the temptation to lust doesn't originate with our eyes but seemingly just pops into our heads. You might be lying in bed or daydreaming in class when all of a sudden a lustful thought pops into your mind out of nowhere. Now what are you going to do? Your key words: *recognize* and *replace.*

Once again, the initial thought is only temptation and not sin. But dwelling on it or entertaining the thought further would be sin. So here's your plan: *Recognize* the thought for what it is, and then immediately *replace* it with a verse of Scripture.

Replace the tempting thought with a verse like this:

> For this is the will of God, your sanctification: that you should abstain from sexual immorality; that each of you should know how to possess his own vessel in sanctification and honor, not in passion of lust, like the Gentiles who do not know God. 1 Thessalonians 4:3–5

Here's another good "replacer" verse:

> Finally, brethren, whatever things are true, whatever things are noble, whatever things are just, whatever things are pure, whatever things are lovely, whatever things are of good report, if there is any virtue and if there is anything praiseworthy—meditate on these things. Philippians 4:8

You can only think one thought at a time. Jesus himself, when tempted three times by Satan, recognized and replaced each temptation with a verse of Scripture. Satan would tempt Him, and Jesus would immediately reply, "It is written . . ." It sounds simple, but it absolutely works! Of course, you must have previously memorized specific passages of God's Word to do this. We will devote more time to this important resource in a later chapter.

The Bible says that our minds are a battlefield. Satan, his demons, and everything in this sinful world wage a constant war for control of our minds. Remember, all sin originates in the mind, so it is no accident the battle rages there so furiously.

The apostle Paul pinpoints the battle and the key to victory:

> For the weapons of our warfare are not carnal but mighty in God for pulling down strongholds, casting down arguments and every high thing that exalts itself against the knowledge of God, bringing every thought into captivity to the obedience of Christ. 2 Corinthians 10:4–5

This battle isn't merely external, it's internal. Just as soldiers diligently protect a fort from attack, *you need to guard your mind from lustful thoughts by recognizing them and replacing them immediately.* You need to take every thought captive and make sure it is in obedience to Jesus Christ.

4. Don't feed your flesh. The Bible compares sexual immorality to a raging fire—if you get too close to it, you will get burned.

> Can a man take fire to his bosom, and his clothes not be burned? Can one walk on hot coals, and his feet not be seared? So is he who goes in to his neighbor's wife; whoever touches her shall not be innocent. Proverbs 6:27–29

Sexual immorality rises out of our flesh—that unredeemable part of every person that incites us to sin and lingers until God gives Christians their perfect, glorified bodies in heaven. The flesh yearns to be fed. You must not feed it, though. The less you feed it, the less will be its appetite; the more you feed it, the hungrier it gets.

This is why you must never put yourself in a position that will fan the flames of sexual immorality. This is why you must constantly guard your eyes, ears, and thoughts. This is why you must make no provision for your flesh.

> But put on the Lord Jesus Christ, and *make no provision for the flesh*, to fulfill its lusts. Romans 13:14

Have you ever heard the words to this old Sunday school song?

Be careful little eyes what you see,
Be careful little ears what you hear,
Be careful little mouth what you say,
Be careful little feet where you go;
For the Father up above is looking down in love,
Oh, be careful little eyes what you see.

In college you might be tempted to *see* movies and television with sexual content or look at Internet pornography. You might be tempted to *hear* sexual gossip and off-color jokes. You might be tempted to *talk* about who's doing what with whom or the lack of clothes a certain person is wearing. You might be tempted to *go* to a strip club or on a morally corrupt spring break trip. Forget "might" . . . you *will* be faced with the choice of serving your own fleshly desires rather than serving God in college.

If you're serious about being morally pure, stay away from the fire. Never be alone in a private place with your boyfriend or girlfriend; avert your eyes from sensual sights on campus, in movies, on television, on billboards, on the Internet; deafen your ears to carnal conversations; filter every thought that comes in your mind. Sexual immorality is powerful and addicting—you must *radically* restrain your fleshly desires.

Yes, God promises to provide a way of escape in the midst of temptation. But when we rush past the escape route He provides, we are then on our own and will fail. Stop trying to see how close you can get to the fire without being burned; rather, keep plenty of distance. *Keep your flesh and your passions cool.* Your intentions may be good, but the intentions of Satan and your flesh are not. Do yourself a big favor— make no provision for your flesh.

5. Flee! There is one sin that is so powerful, so dangerous, and so serious that God doesn't even want you to face it. That sin is sexual immorality, and God commands you to flee!

Man after man, woman after woman, generation after generation have been destroyed by this first Pillar of Peril. No doubt, sexual immorality is Satan's favorite tool of destruction.

The only sure way to deal with this temptation is to run away, remove yourself . . . flee!

> Flee sexual immorality. Every sin that a man does is outside the body, but he who commits sexual immorality sins against his own body. 1 Corinthians 6:18

Remember Joseph? He literally fled from Potiphar's wife, leaving his coat in her hand. Remember King David? He lingered and got burned. I can't say it any more simply: Flee sexual immorality!

We as humans are very *situation sensitive.* In other words, our circumstances deeply affect how we act. Go watch your favorite team win the game, and no doubt you'll be excited. Attend a funeral and no doubt you'll be sober and subdued. Put yourself in a sexually charged environment, and you'll be stimulated.

This is why I strongly recommend that you *not* live in the ultra-promiscuous environs of a co-ed dorm or fraternity/sorority (or go on a party-till-you-drop spring break trip). Keep away from these lascivious domains—live elsewhere with another Christian, a local family, or even at home, and you'll avoid being sullied or desensitized by the full brunt of campus debauchery. Flee, and you'll be free.

6. Dress with discretion. Guys, make it easier for the girls, and girls especially, make it easier for the guys. Since sexual immorality is so rooted in images—both visual and imaginary—the Possessor should dress with discretion and modesty. In other words, dress for success, not for *sex*cess.

> I desire therefore that . . . women adorn themselves in modest apparel, with propriety and moderation . . . which is proper for women professing godliness, with good works. 1 Timothy 2:8–10

Resist the faulty reasoning that "I should be able to wear whatever I want and it's up to others to control their thoughts" or "If you've got it, flaunt it."

Ever seen a beautiful girl who dresses seductively? Want to know what the Bible says about her? "As a ring of gold in a swine's snout, so is a lovely woman who lacks discretion" (Proverbs 11:22). No one would ever put a gold ring in a pig's nose; neither should a lovely woman put indiscreet clothes on her body.

All right, so you want to know specifics—what does it mean to dress with discretion and modesty? *It means you never wear anything that would cause someone's gaze to stray from your face or countenance.* No, I'm not talking burlap sacks here. I'm talking about short skirts, skin-tight pants or shorts, hugging tops, bare midriffs, plunging necklines, or just plain old lots of skin showing. But why am I telling you? You know it when you see it. The same goes for guys. Believe me, the opposite sex will see your beauty even more when you dress with discretion and modesty—they'll only be distracted from it when you dress indiscreetly.

Dress with class and you'll attract classy guys or girls. Dress for *sex*cess and you'll attract all the wrong people with the wrong motives. You've heard the expression "You are what you eat." Well, you are what you *wear*, too. The clothes we wear send a powerful message to others—your responsibility is to dress in such a way that the message can't be misinterpreted.

These are your six keys to overcoming the first Pillar of Peril:

1. Commit to moral purity.
2. Guard your eyes.
3. Guard your thoughts.
4. Don't feed your flesh.
5. Flee!
6. Dress with discretion.

Let me close this chapter by stating that the first Pillar of Peril you will face in college is one tough obstacle. And God has one high standard:

> But fornication and all uncleanness or covetousness, let it not even be named among you, as is fitting for saints; neither filthiness, nor foolish talking, nor coarse jesting, which are not fitting, but rather giving of thanks. Ephesians 5:3–4

God clearly does not want Christians to be linked to any form of sexual immorality because He knows the danger and wants what is best for us. Moral purity is a beautiful thing with mental, spiritual, emotional, and physical benefits and blessings. Moral *im*purity is simply destructive.

Unfortunately, there is not one Christian who is immune to sexual immorality—there are too many examples to prove this point. As a matter of fact, Satan relishes pulling Christians into sexual sin. It gives him a good laugh. Sadly, many Christians entering college—even Christian colleges—will stumble and fall to this first Pillar of Peril.

Yet the Possessor will overcome because he relies upon two all-powerful resources—the indwelling Holy Spirit and the Word of God. The Holy Spirit will *recognize* sexual temptation and gently remind you to *replace* the temptation with the truth of the Word of God. If you listen and obey, this is your unstoppable game plan for victory.

VERY IMPORTANT PRINCIPLE:

The temporary pleasures of sexual sin are not worth offending God and the enduring consequences.

MESSAGE TO MEMORIZE:

Flee sexual immorality. Every sin that a man does is outside the body, but he who commits sexual immorality sins against his own body. 1 CORINTHIANS 6:18

PERSONAL COMMITMENT:

With the power accessible to me through the indwelling Holy Spirit and the Word of God, I will be morally pure in thought and deed. I will also wait to have sex until marriage.

Signature:

Date:

6. THE DATING GAME

The "Mrs." degree—don't leave college without one!

While the *completion* of this "degree" was more common in previous generations, the path to achieve it has remained the same—*dating* is, and will always be, the big game on campus.

We're taking this interlude now because dating and the first Pillar of Peril share plenty of common threads. For the Christian, dating and moral purity should go hand in hand. Unfortunately, this is not always the case. Aside from sexual immorality, the dating game is often characterized by emotional turmoil, academic distraction, broken hearts, parental conflict, petty jealousy, vicious revenge, and even physical abuse. The game can be nasty.

Just as problematic, many Christians continue right on struggling with hurtful dating relationships after college into their twenties, thirties, and forties. Worst of all, marriage doesn't solve the problem—there is very little difference in the divorce rate of Christian couples and non-Christian couples. Something is seriously wrong with this picture.

So what is the problem? Better yet, what is the solution? And most important, how can you avoid being *relationship roadkill* in college? Read on.

Before we talk dating, let's glance ahead at marriage. Just as God designed sex for marriage, He designed marriage primarily for companionship and procreation. If a man and woman choose to marry, the divine standard is that they stay married "until death do us part." But just as sinful man perverted sex to include all the immoral manifestations outside of marriage, so man has done the exact same thing with marriage. Marriage is no longer "until death do us part," but rather "until something gets in the way" or "until someone better comes along."

It should come as no surprise because this is exactly what the dating game has *trained* men and women to do. Here's the typical scenario: A man and woman start dating, but things just don't work out, so they break up. Then they each start dating someone else, but in time they lose interest, so they break up again. The next time around, they're sure they have found Mr. or Miss Right but then meet someone else who seems even more like Mr. or Miss Right, so they end up breaking up again. Get the picture?

As they cycle through one relationship after another, they could be having premarital sex, living together, bearing children out of wedlock, or having abortions. It's all part of the dirty little secret of the dating game.

But then the stars finally align! They find that "perfect person." They have a grand wedding. Everyone is smiling. Married life is great. Perhaps they have kids. They live in a nice home.

Unfortunately, the inevitable occurs. Life happens—financial problems, all-consuming careers, child-raising challenges, interfering in-laws, long business trips, alcohol abuse, another "love" interest . . . and the list goes on.

What do they do? Well, what did they *train* themselves to do during the dating game? If things weren't working out, or if it didn't feel right, or if there was a better option, or if they didn't love each other anymore, they broke up. They got through lost love before; they can get through it again.

So they break up, which in this case means they get divorced. And then they jump back into the dating game and start the whole cycle over again. It is really no wonder that more than 50 percent of marriages (Christian and non-Christian) end in divorce. They're all playing the same losing game . . . the dating game!

DIVINE DATING

What's a guy or gal to do? Is there a way to date but not get caught up in the game? The answer is yes, but you must abide by a complete set of standards that are contrary to the culture, the media, your peers, and even your own desires and feelings.

You must commit to following five fundamental principles of a different kind of dating. What kind of dating is that? *Divine dating.*

Date to Marry

To avoid the repetitive and destructive cycle of the dating game, your perspective on dating must go beyond enjoyment, fulfillment, and romance. Yes, dating can be exhilarating, comforting, loving, and many other things, but that should not be the primary purpose of a dating relationship. Dating for the sake of the little picture (i.e., the benefits) is a sure way to miss out on the big picture (i.e., a good marriage).

Dating should have one primary purpose—marriage. In other words, *date only someone you can envision yourself potentially marrying someday.* "But wait," you say. "How will I ever know if I want to marry someone if I don't date them?" I'm glad you asked. My answer is *look before you leap.*

You've heard the expression "Love is blind." Ain't that the truth! Once you get emotionally involved in a dating relationship, your ability to see the situation clearly drastically declines. Everyone around you may see you are in a relationship with someone who is not right for you, but you are totally blind to it. So you carry on and set yourself up for a big hurt down the road. Then, after it's over, you ask yourself, "What on earth was I thinking?"

Your *one chance* to see a person clearly is *before* the dating relationship begins. This is what I mean when I say, "Look before you leap." Ask yourself the following questions before you start dating:

- "Do we share the same beliefs and values?"
- "What is this person's character?"
- "Would this person be a good father or mother?"
- "Would my family like this person and do I like his or her family?"
- "What are this person's goals and ambitions?"
- "Do we have some common interests?"

- "Can I envision myself married to this person for the rest of my life?"

Answering these questions will take some time and perhaps a few dates. If you come up with several negative answers to the questions, save yourself the misery and don't get involved. If you come up with plenty of positives, proceed ahead, but with your eyes wide open.

The point is to guard your heart before jumping into a dating relationship. Make your decision to date based on sound mental reasoning rather than on just emotion. Ask others who know you best—your parents and close friends—for their opinion and counsel. And don't forget to pray and ask God for discernment. Remember, once you're emotionally entwined, becoming untangled is like taking gum out of your hair—there's no easy and painless way.

This is not dating for the sake of dating. This is dating for the sake of marriage.

Possessors Only, Please

Did you notice the first question to ask yourself about a potential marriage partner: *"Do we share the same beliefs and values?"* In other words, "Does this person share my Christian faith?" This is by far the most important foundation for a dating relationship and marriage.

Who you are as a person is defined by your thoughts, actions, and motives. Guess what dictates your thoughts, actions, and motives? Your spiritual beliefs. If you are a possessing Christian, your thoughts, actions, and motives are going to directly align with the teachings and principles of the Bible.

How does this relate to dating? In every way! A Possessor will be committed to sexual purity before marriage because that is God's will. He will be truthful and aboveboard because that is God's will. She will desire the best for the other person in the relationship because that is God's will. He will raise children with love and discipline because that is God's will. She will prioritize daily Bible study and Christian fellowship because that is God's will.

And last, but not least, he will only date—and thus marry—another Christian because that is God's will:

Do not be unequally yoked together with unbelievers. For

what fellowship has righteousness with lawlessness? And what communion has light with darkness? And what accord has Christ with Belial [Satan]? Or what part has a believer with an unbeliever? And what agreement has the temple of God with idols? For you are the temple of the living God. . . .

Therefore "Come out from among them and be separate, says the Lord. Do not touch what is unclean, and I will receive you." 2 Corinthians 6:14–17

This short passage says a lot. The apostle Paul makes the point that believers and unbelievers are completely different beings—different *animals*, if you will. The "unequal yoke" represents a farmer who tries to plow his field with a donkey and an ox under the same yoke. It just won't work—they'll never plow straight lines because they have completely different *natures*.

According to this passage, God considers believers to be righteous, light, Christ-followers, and His temple. What union could a believer have with an unbeliever whom God considers to be just the opposite— lawless, dark, Satan-followers, and idol worshipers? There are only two "families"—God's and Satan's. Everyone is a member of one or the other, and they don't mix at all. A very stark contrast indeed.

And God's command is clear: "Come out from among them and be separate." Don't date or marry a non-Christian! The apostle Paul reiterates this point in 1 Corinthians 7:29, where he says a Christian should only marry *in the Lord*. In other words, Possessors should marry only other Possessors.

I know what you might be thinking: "Wait a second, I am going to help my non-Christian boyfriend or girlfriend so he or she can become a Christian." For the one case where this actually occurs, there are 999 examples where the opposite happens—the Christian is almost always pulled down spiritually by the non-Christian.

Now, of course, believers must have acquaintances and friendships with unbelievers—Christians are to be salt and light in this dark world. But dating and marriage relationships are much deeper than mere acquaintances or friendships. Go ahead and pray for that person. Invite him or her to church or Bible study. Just don't date or marry that person unless he or she truly becomes a Possessor.

"Missionary dating" is not just a bad idea, it's a spiritually dangerous one. Remember the verse—Christians should not be "unequally yoked" with non-Christians. God's will is that Christians date, and thus marry, only Christians.

Check Your Appearance

All right, so you have found another Christian whom you can envision yourself potentially marrying someday. You start dating. Now what?

You check your appearance.

What does that mean?

The apostle Paul wrote that Christians should "abstain from every form of evil" (1 Thessalonians 5:22).

Avoiding every form (literally "appearance") of evil means that you don't give anyone else grounds to think something sinful is going on in your relationship.

God wants not only purity in your dating relationship but purity in the *appearance* of your relationship too. You see, God is very protective of His name, His holiness, His reputation. He doesn't want those who say they represent Him (i.e., Christians) appearing to behave in such a way that would tarnish His reputation.

This means you must conduct your dating relationship to a much higher standard than unbelievers do. If people see you and your dating partner hugging and smooching in the hallway, you are giving them reason to think, "If they are doing that in public, I can only imagine what they are doing in private." Or if they see you drive off together for a little weekend getaway, they're going to think, "Hmm, hot nights ahead for those two."

The reality might be that everything is aboveboard with you and your dating partner, but you are giving the appearance that it is not. Of course, some people will suspect sin due to the mere fact that you're dating, but never give them any appearance to confirm their wandering imaginations.

"Flesh, you're fired."

As you read in the last chapter, our unredeemed flesh pulls powerfully against us. There is a literal war going on inside a Christian between the flesh and the Spirit. This is heightened even more in a dating relationship, and Satan will ignite your flesh to work overtime to destroy your testimony for Jesus Christ. He will try to pervert the love you are building with each other by tempting you to do things against God's will.

So you must make no provision for your flesh with your dating partner. Never be alone with each other in a dorm room. Never stay together when traveling. Never spend time in a deserted place—even outside—especially at night. In short, *never put yourself in a private situation that could be conducive to moral impurity.* Period.

This applies to not only your dating partner but anyone of the opposite sex. I know many godly men and women who make no provision for their flesh by upholding this principle.

More than any other sin, sexual immorality often occurs suddenly and unexpectedly because it is fueled by passion and emotion, which can spike in a moment. Read how a young man is seduced by a woman in the book of Proverbs:

> For at the window of my house I looked through my lattice, and saw among the simple, I perceived among the youths, a young man devoid of understanding, passing along the street near her corner; and he took the path to her house in the twilight, in the evening, in the black and dark night. . . . Immediately he went after her, as an ox goes to the slaughter. . . . He did not know it would cost his life. Proverbs 7:6–9, 22–23

For this young man sexual immorality happened suddenly ("immediately") and unexpectedly ("devoid of understanding"). Yet he is without excuse. He made provision for his flesh. He went to her house at night. His flesh overpowered him and it cost him his life.

How far is too far?

While we're on this topic, let's clear up an issue that is often debated by unmarried Christian couples: Where is God's line between sexual purity and sexual immorality? Is everything short of sexual intercourse okay? Is oral sex permissible? Can we take our clothes off and touch each other's bodies? What about hugging, or kissing with the tongue? Or hand holding? Is that wrong?

I'll let you answer the question: *Can you romantically touch another person's body without breaking God's commands to abstain from every appearance of evil and to make no provision for your flesh?*

If you're honest, the answer is no. Those who say that God permits anything besides sexual intercourse are only rationalizing and deluding themselves. Remember, to God a lustful thought is the same as a sinful act. No one can intimately touch another person's body without lust entering the mind. I believe God wants unmarried Christian couples to stay on the side of holding hands or a "non-invasive" kiss . . . and wait until marriage for the rest.

Parental Approval

Far and away, the second most important decision you will ever make in life is whom you marry. (Whether you believe in Jesus Christ as Savior and Lord is the first.) The saying goes that whom you marry determines 95 percent of your happiness in life . . . or 95 percent of your misery! Perhaps a bit overstated, but you get the point.

Can you name all of the Ten Commandments? The one that people invariably forget is number five:

> Honor your father and your mother, so that your days may be long upon the land which the Lord your God is giving you. Exodus 20:12

The apostle Paul repeated the command in the New Testament:

> "Honor your father and mother," which is the first commandment with promise: that it may be well with you and that you may live long on the earth. Ephesians 6:2–3

When you're divinely dating, make sure you seek and listen to those who know you best and want the best for you, namely, your parents.

What we're really talking about here is utilizing your God-given authorities. Notice that I said *utilizing* and not *resenting*. God has designed a structure of authority to protect us from getting off course and to direct us down the right road. Submit to your God-given authorities and you are blessed; resist and you are on your own—unprotected and undirected. It's a simple equation.

God has ordained four structures of authority: parents over children, government over citizens, church leaders over believers, and employers over employees. He wants everyone, and I mean everyone, to willingly submit to these authorities.

Most people strongly resist being under authority because it goes against our human pride. "I will make my own decisions; I will be the master of my own ship; I won't let anyone tell me what to do!"

So they pay the price. Ask a divorced person sometime if their parents wholeheartedly approved of their marriage. My anecdotal poll says that the answer is invariably no. (Some will say their parents didn't care, and in that case, shame on the parents for not giving counsel on such a major decision!) To the contrary, you will have a difficult time finding a divorced couple where both sets of parents gave their wholehearted approval.

So what does this have to do with dating? Everything. You have found another Christian you can envision yourself marrying, you are committed to abstaining from every form of evil, and now it's time to get some counsel from your parents. *Get it early!*

Before you become so emotionally attached that it would be difficult to let go, make a special point to introduce the person to your parents. Spend time together with your own family. Spend time together with your dating partner's family.

If after plenty of interaction your parents have major problems with your choice of a dating partner, you had better take their warning very seriously. To "honor" means you make every effort to obey. That is why I say get your parents involved early rather than a week before the wedding.

What if your parents are divorced, not believers, or you have a highly dysfunctional family? These situations will take some discernment on your part. Unless you sense your parents are intentionally provoking and trying to hurt you, do everything you can to honor them. But you may need to seek out counsel from your church leaders if a parental problem persists.

Remember, use your parents to protect you from dating and marrying the wrong person and to help direct you to date and marry the right person.

Triangulate!

And then it happens. There you are in a divine dating relationship. Finally—true love at last! You've found your soul mate. Parents on both sides approve. Wedding bells are ringing in your head. You're imagining sunset strolls on the beach, your first home, 2.3 children. Life is good.

Don't forget to *triangulate!*

What on earth does that mean? It means to remember to include the most important Person in your divine dating relationship—Jesus Christ. It means to form a virtual hand-holding triangle with Him and your boyfriend or girlfriend. Keep one hand reserved for Christ and the other reserved for your dating partner.

A natural tendency in dating (and marriage) can be to get your eyes totally focused on the other person, to the exclusion of your more important relationship with Christ. Or worse yet, you can get overly focused on yourself, expecting your dating partner to fulfill your deepest needs. No human being can or should be expected to do that. Expecting this is a recipe for a ruined relationship. Only your relationship with Jesus Christ can fulfill your every need; only He can make you complete . . . not another person.

> For in Him dwells all the fullness of the Godhead bodily; and you are complete in Him, who is the head of all principality and power. Colossians 2:9–10

Besides, do you know what God calls a relationship where a couple has eyes only for each other? *Idolatry.* Idolatry is putting *anyone,* such as a boyfriend or girlfriend, or *anything,* such as education, career, sports, recreation, and possessions, ahead of your relationship with Christ. It is putting one of these "gods" ahead of the true God.

And, oh boy, does God hate idolatry. He won't stand for anyone or anything taking His rightful place. Even the closest human relationships must come second to our love for Him. If not, the Bible says He will be "jealous":

> For you shall worship no other god, for the Lord, whose name is Jealous, is a jealous God. Exodus 34:14

So form your triangle with your dating partner and Jesus Christ by keeping your relationship with Him in first place. Some practical ways to do this with your boyfriend or girlfriend are to study the Bible together, attend church together, memorize a passage of Scripture together, and pray together. Whether single or coupled, God wants believers to seek His kingdom and His righteousness first before anyone or anything else.

> But seek first the kingdom of God and His righteousness, and
> all these things shall be added to you. Matthew 6:33

One final benefit of forming a triangle is that you will soon discover the true spiritual condition of your dating partner. If, in time, you find his or her spiritual life lacking and don't detect any motivation to change, you might come to the conclusion that he or she is not the right one for you. On the other hand, if you discover someone who is motivated to grow spiritually, this will confirm and give you confidence that you are on the right track with the right person.

And what about those sunset walks on the beach with just the two of you? Make room for three!

>—•—<

So, what have you learned about dating? First, forget the dating game so prevalent on college campuses today. Almost everyone plays the game, and it only trains them for future disaster.

Rather, commit to divine dating:

- Date to marry.
- Possessors only, please.
- Check your appearance.
- Parental approval.
- Triangulate!

Even if you follow this plan, your first divine dating relationship may not end up in marriage. You may find out things later about the person you don't like; you may discover the person is a professing rather than possessing Christian; you may find out the person does not want moral purity; or you may find your parents have sound objections to the relationship.

Be comforted, though. God knows your heart—He knows you went about it the right way. You made the best decisions you could at the time. You were obedient to Him. You didn't compromise yourself morally and are still saving yourself for the right one someday. You weren't indiscriminately playing the dating game; you were dating with a purpose.

Just wait on the Lord . . . for in God's time, it will be truly *divine*.

VERY IMPORTANT PRINCIPLE:

Out with the dating game, in with divine dating!

MESSAGE TO MEMORIZE:

Do not be unequally yoked together with unbelievers. . . . [And only date and marry] in the Lord. 2 CORIN-
THIANS 6:14; 1 CORINTHIANS 7:39

7. SECOND PILLAR OF PERIL— DRUGS AND ALCOHOL

"Eat, drink, and be merry, for tomorrow . . . *we do it all over again!*"

The parties never stop in college, and neither do the primary lubricants—drugs and alcohol. It certainly won't be necessary to BYOA to college—why **B**ring **Y**our **O**wn **A**lcohol, or drugs for that matter, when they will be so easily accessible on campus?

It is hardly an exaggeration to say that the all-too-common existence of many college students is living from one drunken stupor to the next. Drive around campus some Friday or Saturday evening, and you will find students partying until the wee hours. And don't waste your time trying to find a reason for the reveling—this is just college life, and getting drunk or high is the name of the game.

Tragically, Christians on campus are not immune. Plenty of Christian college students get sucked in and flattened by this second Pillar of Peril. What starts out as "just a drink" turns into social drinking, which turns into drunkenness, which turns into a ruined testimony for God—not to mention the regret and shame of things done while intoxicated or, worse, a crippling or life-ending accident.

And, as usual, Satan always tempts by showing the attractive beginning of the way but never the bitter end. He will show you the "fun" but never the consequence. Consider this powerful passage from Proverbs (freely interchanging "beer" for "wine"):

> Who has woe? Who has sorrow? Who has contentions? Who has complaints? Who has wounds without cause? Who has redness of eyes? Those who linger long at the wine, those who go in search of mixed wine. Do not look on the wine when it is red, when it sparkles in the cup, when it swirls around smoothly; at the last it bites like a serpent, and stings like a viper. Your eyes will see strange things, and your heart will utter perverse things. Yes, you will be like one who lies down in the midst of the sea, or like one who lies at the top of the mast, saying: "They have struck me, but I was not hurt; they have beaten me, but I did not feel it. When shall I awake, that I may seek another drink?" Proverbs 23:29–35

Sound like a campus near you?

You would think with all the negative consequences of drug use and alcohol abuse—stubborn addictions, declining physical and mental health, ruined families and relationships, unintended pregnancies—that young people would shy away from the party life. Yet there exists almost an irresistible attraction to what has destroyed countless lives, generation after generation.

The perils of drug and alcohol abuse are definitely not unique to college campuses, nor to modern times. The Old Testament story of Abraham's nephew, Lot, impregnating his two daughters while intoxicated and passages in the New Testament prohibiting drunkenness prove that this Pillar of Peril is nothing new. The Bible speaks very clearly on this topic. The apostle Paul wrote to Christians:

> And do not be drunk with wine, in which is dissipation [squandering your life]; but be filled with the Spirit. Ephesians 5:18

What's the command? *Don't be drunk.* It's as simple as that.

Did you notice the *reason* why we are not to be drunk, though? There is a contrast in this verse, an either/or statement. Let me paraphrase the verse: "Don't be drunk, but instead, be filled with the Holy Spirit." In other words, either you are drunk and not filled with the Spirit, or you are sober and you can be filled with the Spirit.

It is interesting—and descriptive—to note that alcohol is often called "spirits"—we can be filled with either alcoholic "spirits" or the Holy Spirit . . . but not both.

As we have learned, if you are a Possessor, there is an ongoing war inside you between the Spirit and that unredeemed part of you—your flesh. When you are sober, you can be filled with the Spirit. But anytime you are drunk or high, you will be controlled by your flesh and act out its sinful desires. Which explains why drinking almost invariably precedes sex on campus—the first inevitability leads to the second.

This is exactly the intended purpose and reason behind why people use drugs or get drunk—they want to feed their flesh because it feels good and helps them temporarily escape the reality of their *Spirit-less* existence.

One can *never* be fully content without possessing what truly satisfies: the indwelling Holy Spirit, which stems from a relationship with God through Jesus Christ. Those who don't possess the Spirit end up trying to fill their inner spiritual vacuum with drugs or drink (or sex, amusement, money, other religions, etc.). They are not Possessors of the Holy Spirit and, therefore, do not bear the following fruit of the indwelling Spirit:

> But the fruit of the Spirit is love, joy, peace, longsuffering, kindness, goodness, faithfulness, gentleness, self-control. Galatians 5:22–23

Only the Spirit can produce this fruit. Many thousands of students go through college without godly love, divine joy, lasting peace, and self-control. Being void of the Spirit and His fruit, mere Professors and unbelievers are enslaved to their flesh and are characterized by a life of sinful thoughts, actions, and motives. This is why so many young people are unhappy and discontented, resulting in depression and even suicide.

Let's face it, the only reason people take drugs—whether it's smoking marijuana, snorting cocaine, injecting heroin, popping pills—is to alter their state of mind. They want to escape their present reality.

Alcohol is not much different. College students drink alcohol for one reason and one reason only—to lessen their inhibition to sin. They are certainly not just thirsty; otherwise, they'd drink a couple glasses of water! No, they drink beer, wine, and mixed drinks in order to loosen up, to forget their inner emptiness, to break the ice with the opposite sex, to feel good for a moment . . . to feed their flesh. It's their first step toward "fun."

Peers and Beers

Let's not discount the "peer factor" either. College students (and older people for that matter) drink because there is a subtle pressure by their peers and society. Many people would feel totally out of place at a party or gathering without a drink in their hand. Other people wouldn't even attend a party if there wasn't alcohol served—"No alcohol, no go" is their motto.

Everyone wants to be liked and accepted; it's human nature. Peer pressure is often strongest during the teenage and young adult years. No one wants to feel like an outcast, so they do what everyone else is doing. It seems simplistic, but it's true.

And then there is the cultural pressure. Drinking wine or mixed drinks has the aura of being mature and sophisticated, while drinking beer has the implication of being fun. Think how they are marketed— hard liquor companies show a well-dressed man and woman eyeing each other in a sophisticated environment, while beer companies show guys and girls whooping it up at the bar or at the game.

Of course, companies never display the downsides to drinking in their ads, do they? They don't show the hangovers, the car accidents, the ruined lives, or any of the other perils mentioned.

Now, you know that drugs and alcohol are a menacing threat on college campuses, even to Christians. You even know why people get seduced by them. The question that remains is, how are you going to steer clear of this Pillar of Peril? How are you going to be an Overcomer?

To Beer or Not to Beer

You've probably noticed that I have been specific in writing drug *use* and alcohol *abuse*. All drug use, except for legitimate medicinal purposes, is clearly wrong because it alters your spiritual state. You can't be high on drugs and at the same time be filled with the Holy Spirit.

But what about alcohol? The Bible says "be not drunk," because, like drug use, it alters your spiritual state. But what about having a beer or glass of wine? Is that wrong? Is it okay to drink if you don't get intoxicated?

First, let me give you a simple answer: It is absolutely wrong to drink alcohol if you are under the legal drinking age because you would be breaking the law. God commands Christians to be obedient to the laws of our government. If you willfully break this law, you are thumbing your nose at God's ordained authority.

The underage law may cover you for now, but that is only a temporary external restraint. We all know the drinking age is often circumvented and not enforced on campus. This bigger question is this: Should you drink, even if you are of age?

Before answering that, let's consider one more thing.

A Beer in Front of Your Peers?

Do you remember the biblical principle emphasized in the last two chapters that Christians are to "avoid every appearance of evil"? How does that apply to drinking? Well, it changes the question from "Is drinking permissible?" to the more important question, "Would drinking negatively affect my Christian testimony to others?"

For example, if you stood from a distance and watched a party at a fraternity or campus bar where people were drinking heavily, what would you think? You'd think, "Now, there is a sinful environment, a den of drunkenness." And you'd be exactly right.

Now what if you, as a Christian, are in the midst of that same party when someone else stands outside and observes the identical scene? What appearance are you giving that person? Even if you're sober, you are giving the appearance that you are one of them, one of the drunken members of the carousing crowd. You may have had one drink and be completely sober, but by associating with this crowd, you are giving the appearance that you are part of the sin that is taking place. You have not avoided every appearance of evil; you are in the midst of it.

But it gets worse. Let's say that person standing outside is a new Christian and sees you, a more mature Christian, in the midst of that party. What is that new Christian going to think? At best, he or she will be confused by your being involved with a group of drunken, carousing partiers. At worst, he or she will think that if you're there, it must be okay to partake in this type of activity. You are then responsible for potentially leading this new Christian right into the second Pillar of Peril. Don't believe me? Consider this verse:

> But whoever causes one of these little ones [new Christians] who believe in Me to stumble, it would be better for him if a millstone were hung around his neck, and he were thrown into the sea. Mark 9:42

God says that if you cause another believer to stumble into sin because of your actions, it would be better for you to be drowned!

We may have the liberty to drink, but not when it gives the appearance of evil or causes another Christian to stumble. Many people associate drinking alcohol with sin, and right or wrong, you must defer to their conscience, not your own. Read this passage and substitute "drinking alcohol" for "eating in an idol's temple."

> But beware lest somehow this liberty of yours become a stumbling block to those who are weak. For if anyone sees you who have knowledge eating in an idol's temple, will not the conscience of him who is weak be emboldened to eat those things offered to idols? And because of your knowledge shall the weak brother perish, for whom Christ died? But when you thus sin against the brethren, and wound their weak conscience, you sin against Christ. Therefore, if food makes my brother stumble, I will never again eat meat [or drink alcohol], lest I make my brother stumble. 1 Corinthians 8:9–13

The principle here is that we must always consider how our actions will affect the conscience of others. If there is the slightest chance that drinking alcohol would negatively influence the conscience of another Christian or bring disrepute upon the name of Christ, we must not partake!

Final Call for Alcohol?

Now let's answer this question: Should you drink even if you are of age?

I'll frame my answer in a challenge to you: Commit to a higher standard—*don't drink alcohol . . . period!* Take it out of play; remove it completely from your life. Are you willing to make this commitment—

a commitment that will save you from hurting yourself, others, and God?

For the life of me, I can think of no positive reasons for drinking alcoholic beverages. Even on a purely financial level, drinking is very expensive. Many, many people blow their paycheck every weekend on alcohol. At a typical bar, a beer is usually three or more dollars and a glass of wine even higher. That much hard-earned cash for a beverage? Think of all the money you could save by *not* drinking alcohol! Even if it's free, it's still not worth the "price."

"But I like the taste of wine or beer," you say. Understood. But there are so many other non-alcoholic beverages to choose from that taste plenty good too—soft drinks, juices, teas, coffee. People who don't drink alcohol get by just fine. Alcohol is definitely not a need.

With all the potential serious consequences—drunkenness, alcoholism, health problems, broken relationships, career endangerment, pregnancy complications, car accidents, immoral behavior—it makes one ask, "Is drinking really worth the risk?" The answer is a resounding NO! Talk to anyone who has been leveled by alcohol abuse and they will tell you the same thing.

If you are currently trying, using, or entangled in drug use or alcohol abuse, you need to change course and get help right away—from your parents, your youth group leader, a medical professional, school counselor . . . anyone! And I'm not just talking to so-called drug addicts or alcoholics (most people won't ever admit they are one). I'm talking to anyone who is dabbling with drugs and alcohol but wants to overcome this Pillar of Peril.

Just as important, confess your sin to God and ask Him to take you in a whole new direction. Whenever you are tempted, replace the thought with this verse: "Do not be drunk with wine [alcohol or drugs] . . . but be filled with the Spirit" (Ephesians 5:18).

There is only one sure way to overcome this second Pillar of Peril: Stay away from drugs and alcohol altogether! Period. End of story. Don't experiment or ever use drugs. Make a commitment to be alcohol free. Grab a Mountain Dew instead of a Miller Lite. Decide beforehand that drugs and alcohol are not going to be a part of your life in college. Steer clear of situations where there is strong temptation to use them and thereby avoid the possibility that you might cause another Christian to be offended or to stumble. Be ready with an answer to anyone who mocks or questions your decision to be drug and alcohol free.

The Pretender will do just that; he will mock those who do not share his yearning for drugs or alcohol. He will personify the verse from Proverbs: "They have struck me, but I was not hurt; they have beaten me, but I did not feel it. When shall I awake, that I may seek another drink?" (Proverbs 23:35).

The Compromiser will say, "A little marijuana or a few drinks never hurt anyone—everyone's doing it; it's just havin' fun." He or she is destined to get "[bitten] like a serpent, [stung] like a viper" (Proverbs 23:32).

The Overcomer, though, will gain victory over this Pillar of Peril because he or she has made a commitment to not displace the indwelling Spirit with a "liquid spirit" or illicit drugs. With the Spirit in, drugs and alcohol are definitely out.

The Overcomer will choose this higher standard. How about you?

VERY IMPORTANT PRINCIPLE:

A Christian under the influence of drugs or alcohol is not under the influence of the Holy Spirit.

MESSAGE TO MEMORIZE:

And do not be drunk with wine, but be filled with the Spirit. EPHESIANS 5:18

PERSONAL COMMITMENT:

I will not use alcohol or drugs in college.

Signature:

Date:

8. UNDER THE INFLUENCE OF . . . MUSIC!

Music matters!

A chapter on music is the perfect connector between the second and third Pillars of Peril.

How so? Do you remember the Message to Memorize from the second Pillar of Peril (drugs and alcohol)? "And do not be drunk with wine, in which is dissipation; but be filled with the Spirit . . ."

You might be surprised what the rest of the verse says: ". . . speaking to one another in *psalms* and *hymns* and *spiritual songs, singing* and making *melody* in your heart to the Lord" (Ephesians 5:18–19).

"Psalms, hymns, spiritual songs, singing, making melody"—it's all about music! Rather than being filled with mind-altering substances, be filled with the Spirit through uplifting *music*. It's interesting that drunkenness is linked, actually *contrasted*, with spiritual music.

All right, that's how music is connected to the second Pillar of Peril; but how does music relate to the third Pillar of Peril ("Rock 'n' Roll")? Remember, the third Pillar of Peril is not rock 'n' roll music specifically, but rather, what rock 'n' roll has traditionally represented—*rebellion 'n' rejection* of God and His Word.

Let me illustrate through a story from the Old Testament how certain music cultivates rebellion 'n' rejection. Moses, the great leader of the Jews' exodus from Egypt, and Joshua, his assistant, were up on Mount Sinai receiving the Ten Commandments from God. Meanwhile, the nation of Israel was busy making and worshiping an idol in the form of a golden calf in their camp at the base of the mountain.

Furthermore, as part of the "worship," the Bible says the people "rose up to play." This is a nice way of saying they were committing gross sexual immorality, dancing sensually, and getting drunk. Read the following account without missing the description of the music accompanying this lewd affair.

> And [Aaron] received the gold from their [people of Israel's] hand, and he fashioned it with an engraving tool, and made a molded calf. Then they said, "This is your god, O Israel, that brought you out of the land of Egypt!" So when Aaron saw it, he built an altar before it.
>
> And Aaron made a proclamation and said, "Tomorrow is a feast to the Lord." Then they rose early on the next day, offered burnt offerings, and brought peace offerings; and the people sat down to eat and drink, and *rose up to play*.
>
> And the Lord said to Moses, "Go, get down! For your people whom you brought out of the land of Egypt have corrupted themselves. They have turned aside quickly out of the way which I commanded them. . . ."
>
> And Moses turned and went down from the mountain, and the two tablets of the Testimony [the Ten Commandments] were in his hand. . . . And when Joshua heard the noise of the people as they shouted, he said to Moses, "There is a *noise of war* in the camp." But he said:
>
> "It is not the noise of the shout of victory,
>
> Nor the noise of the cry of defeat,
>
> But the *sound of singing* I hear."
>
> So it was, as soon as he came near the camp, that he saw the calf and the dancing. So Moses' anger became hot, and he cast the tablets out of his hands and broke them at the foot of the mountain. . . .
>
> Now when Moses saw that the people were unrestrained (for Aaron had not restrained them, to their shame among their enemies), then Moses stood in the entrance of the camp, and said,

"Whoever is on the Lord's side—come to me. . . ." Now it came to pass on the next day that Moses said to the people, "You have committed a great sin." Exodus 32:4–30

Not a pretty scene in the camp of Israel (not unlike some campus parties). The point, though, is that the type of music coming from the camp confused Joshua into thinking there was a war. In reality, the kind of music being played served as an appropriate accompaniment to the people's rebellion 'n' rejection of God.

Music Is Moral

These previous two passages of Scripture convey this important fact about music: There is a *moral* aspect to music. In other words, certain music brings praise to God and inspires righteousness, while other types of music ignite sinful tendencies such as sexual immorality, self-centeredness, or violence. Blindly, many Christians believe all music is neutral—"Music is just a series of notes" or "a matter of preference."

In the first passage from the book of Ephesians, the music—"psalms, hymns, and spiritual songs"—is seen as good, pleasing to God, having a positive effect on Christians, and contrasted to drunkenness.

On the other hand, in the second passage from the book of Exodus, the music—"sound of war," inspiring sensual dance and immorality—is seen as evil, displeasing to God, and having a very negative effect on the people.

The goal of this chapter is to help you discern between spiritual music and sinful music so you can choose music that is glorifying to God and spiritually strengthening to you.

Remember, music is not meaningless—music matters! All music is not created equal; there is righteous music and there is sinful music (and some neutral music in between). Sinful music appeals to our fallen flesh. Spiritual music has the opposite effect—it elevates our spirit. What is dangerous for some Christians is that they base their choice of music on what sounds or feels good or what is popular. This is definitely *not* the criteria on which music should be judged.

If It Sounds Good, Listen to It?

Think about the "it makes me feel good" or "I like the sound" standard and ask yourself the following questions:

- Listening to an off-color comedian may make you laugh, but is it good for your mind?
- Watching a sexual scene in a movie may please your flesh, but is it good for your soul?
- Eating two pints of ice cream every night may taste great at the moment, but is it good for your body?

To all three questions, the answer is, of course not! Just as we have to make the right choices about what we watch with our eyes or put in our mouths, we need to make the right choice about what we listen to with our *ears*.

Speaking of eating, I believe music is actually an *acquired taste*. In other words, when you choose a particular genre of music and listen to it on a regular basis, you will develop an appetite to hear more of the same style. If you feed your flesh with carnal music, its appetite for more will grow. To the contrary, if you feed your spirit with music glorifying to God, your spiritual appetite will grow.

So where are we? First, music is moral—there are rights and wrongs when it comes to music. Second, music is powerful—the type of music a Christian (or anyone) chooses to listen to will have a great impact upon him or her spiritually, emotionally, mentally, and even physically. Third, musical choice should go beyond mere preference, more than just what I like. And last, music is an acquired taste.

I can hear your question: How can you discern between spiritual music and sinful music? There are many different forms of music, numerous musicians, and countless songs from which to choose. How can you choose wisely?

It takes not only a discerning ear but a discerning spirit.

Sound and Words

For those of you who have studied music, you know that it can be quite complex. For instance, any given song has variations in melody, harmony, beat, pitch, timing, and volume. Fundamentally, though, music can be divided into two basic parts—*rhythm* and *lyrics*. Sound and words. Each of these two parts has the ability to communicate a powerful message.

Rhythm is produced by varying melody, harmony, beat, pitch, and timing. It is the *sound* of the music produced by instruments and/or voice.

Lyrics are simply *words* that accompany that sound. Just as rhythm is used to convey the musician's message, lyrics are used to make the message even stronger.

Power, Power, Power!

The power of music lies in its ability to communicate on a much deeper level than speech alone. For instance, when you listen to your professor teach, primarily your intellect is being stimulated. But when you listen to music, not only your mind but your emotions, your will, and your spirit are touched. That is the power of music.

But wait, there's more! Music is even *more* powerful when *sight* is brought into the equation. Carnal (appealing to the flesh) music videos combine not only sound and words but visual scenes with strong sexual overtones that powerfully impact the viewer/listener. No one can watch rappers and their dancers gyrate on screen while singing, "It's gettin' hot in here, so take off all your clothes" without being spiritually sullied. The shtick of Britney Spears and others like her are no exception.

The sensual sounds, suggestive lyrics, and sinful scenes of most secular music videos create a potent audio/visual display. In the old days one had to go to a concert to get this effect, but now one is able to simply turn on the TV. Is it any wonder that MTV, VH1, and BET television networks have so continually coarsened our culture? And if you've noticed, the videos and music produced only get more extreme with each passing year. Elvis Presley's swiveling hips back in the 1950s seem downright tame by today's standards.

Pro-Choice

But as mentioned earlier, you don't have to go with the flow. Just as we have a choice in what we watch on television or with whom we associate, we also have a choice in which kind of music we listen to. This seems obvious, but on most college campuses you would think this isn't the case.

Typically, one variety of music overwhelmingly prevails in college—carnal, worldly music, whether in the form of certain types of rock, rap, or hip-hop, music that has the same impact as it did on the nation of

Israel. Think there's musical diversity on campus? Check out the music in your nearest dorm room, student center, or fitness area. Spiritually uplifting? I don't think so.

Of course, it's not surprising. Do you remember the scene at the fraternity party or campus bar in the last chapter? Ask yourself what kind of music that crowd will want to listen to. In the midst of their partying, do you think they will desire music honoring to God or music that feeds their flesh?

Or do you think non-Christians in general, those not possessing the indwelling Holy Spirit, will gravitate toward music that honors God? Rarely. Just like those who take drugs or use alcohol, they will try to satisfy their spiritual emptiness by listening to what makes them feel good at the moment—they will put themselves under the influence of . . . sinful music.

Or do you think any of the popular musical artists on radio or MTV whose lives are characterized by sinfulness—immorality, rebellion against God—are able to produce anything of redeeming value for Christian ears? Jesus spoke the following to the unbelieving, hypocritical religious leaders of His day, the Pharisees:

> How can you, being evil, speak good things? For out of the abundance of the heart the mouth speaks. A good man out of the good treasure of his heart brings forth good things, and an evil man out of the evil treasure brings forth evil things. Matthew 12:34–35

That sums it up well. Nothing good can come out of a bad heart. Think of prominent past and current musicians like Elvis, the Beatles, the Rolling Stones, Prince, Michael Jackson, Madonna, Britney Spears, Eminem, and Usher. It hardly takes a look beneath the surface to see lives characterized by sin, whether it is sexual promiscuity, drug and alcohol abuse, or rebellion against God's Word.

Here is how they think:

- "Who says it's wrong to have sex outside of marriage? I'll do it with whomever I want and sing about it."
- "Who says it's wrong to take drugs or get drunk? I'll get high and glamorize it in my lyrics."
- "Who says it's wrong to use foul language? I'll sprinkle vulgarity

throughout my songs and use four-letter words on national television."

- "Who says it's wrong to dress and dance seductively? I'll push the envelope whenever I can."

To no surprise, their music mirrors their lives. The sensual sound, the lyrics, and their videos either promote or, at minimum, glamorize their ungodly lifestyle. Their music represents all that Satan and his sinful world system have to offer. Knowing the source and the detrimental effects, a Possessor should choose to not listen to or watch their carnal music, for it only feeds the flesh.

> Do not love the world or the things in the world. If anyone loves the world, the love of the Father is not in him. For all that is in the world—the lust of the flesh, the lust of the eyes, and the pride of life—is not of the Father but is of the world. And the world is passing away, and the lust of it; but he who does the will of God abides forever. 1 John 2:15–17

Carnal music is one part of this sinful world system—man's tendency toward pride, self-sufficiency, and lust for fame, fortune, power, and pleasure make up the other parts. Listen to the world's ungodly music and you will see that it conveys these unrighteous values. For a Christian to listen to it is to compromise, corrupt, and brainwash his own mind to their godless ideology.

Music for Possessors

Enough of the bad, let's look at the good. What type of music should a Christian choose, then? Do you remember the type of music described in the verse at the beginning of this chapter?

> But be filled with the Spirit, speaking to one another in *psalms* and *hymns* and *spiritual songs,* singing and making melody in your heart to the Lord.

Here is the type of music that brings glory to God and strengthens our spirit—psalms and hymns and spiritual songs. We need to find this music and acquire a taste for it.

Psalms

Did you know the book of Psalms was originally intended to be sung? *Psalms* literally means "songs"—Psalms is the songbook of the Bible. The nation of Israel and Christians throughout the ages have sung these verses of Scripture. What could be more uplifting and honoring to God than listening to or singing back to Him His own inspired words?

Hymns

Hymns are songs with a strong spiritual emphasis and biblical basis. They have been sung by Christians throughout the centuries for praise, comfort, and worship. They are characterized by foundational doctrine and theological truth. Sadly, the singing of hymns is disappearing from churches across our country and is being replaced by an almost exclusive focus on a somewhat recent genre broadly termed contemporary Christian music. While there is much contemporary Christian music that is praiseworthy and uplifting (yet some that needs careful consideration, as we'll discuss next), my point is that the hymns that strengthened and inspired Christians for generations shouldn't be forgotten but rather should remain on the lips and in the ears of the younger generation of Christians today.

Spiritual Songs

The last category of godly music is *spiritual songs*. What exactly is a "spiritual song"? A common (and incorrect) definition would be any type of music—whether contemporary, rock, rap, and so on—that has a "Christian message."

But just mentioning God or the joys and struggles of being a Christian in the lyrics—is that what the Bible is referring to as a "spiritual song"? Does the rhythm or sound of a given song matter at all, even if it has Christian lyrics? I think it does.

In order to discern what truly defines a spiritual song, let's identify the qualities that both the lyrics and rhythm should have to be congruent with Scripture.

First of all, a spiritual song must have spiritual content in the *lyrics*. The words of the song must convey sound biblical truth about God, Jesus Christ, and the Holy Spirit or be a response of praise, worship, or thankfulness for what He has done or is doing (much like a psalm or hymn). The words of spiritual songs should emphasize God and His attributes rather than focus on human-centered issues such as relationship troubles or personal feelings.

You've checked the lyrics for spiritual content; now give the *rhythm* of the music a spiritual sound check. Does the sound of the music arouse any sensual (sexual) or angry feelings or thoughts in your body or mind? Does your body feel like it wants to dance or move in a carnal way? Does the music sound just like the world's music, like something you would hear at that campus bar, a sinful party, or on the radio of one who rebels against God?

Or does the sound of the music direct the focus of your mind, will, emotions, and spirit toward God rather than toward yourself? Does the rhythm of the music inspire your body to move in praise to God without being sexually suggestive to others? Does the sound of the song cause your enlivened spirit to commune with the Holy Spirit?

In short, spiritual songs must have lyrics and rhythm—both words and sound—directed upward at God, not downward at your flesh. When Christian music is self-centered rather than God-centered, it will only serve to stunt your spiritual growth. Perhaps even worse, when lyrics are seemingly spiritual but the rhythm is carnal, inner conflict can be the result. The Spirit and the flesh don't mix.

You have to be *so* discriminating with music in college. Think of world-class athletes—they have to be careful what they eat or drink, what they take into their bodies. It is the same for Christians when it comes to music. Listen to sinful music, and carnality will result. Listen to godly music, and spiritual maturity will result. What applies to our eyes and mouths also applies to our ears.

Music is moral. Music is powerful. Music is a choice. And music is an acquired taste. In college and beyond, choose godly music—*psalms and hymns and spiritual songs.*

Better yet, put yourself *under the influence* of it.

VERY IMPORTANT PRINCIPLE:

Music matters—choose spiritual music over sinful music.

MESSAGE TO MEMORIZE:

Be filled with the Spirit, speaking to one another in psalms and hymns and spiritual songs, singing and making melody in your heart to the Lord. EPHESIANS 5:18–19

9. THIRD PILLAR OF PERIL— "ROCK 'N' ROLL"

Don't believe the Lie!

Some time ago, a young girl named Eve attended the University of Eden. She majored in horticulture (the study of plants, trees, fruits, and vegetables—*gardening*, if you will). For a horticultural major, there was no better place to study than the University of Eden. The campus had such spectacular natural beauty that it made the Ivy League look bush-league in comparison.

Eve was a unique college student. Having no desire to play the dating game, she married an upstanding young man named Adam, who also attended the University of Eden and shared the same major. Being married in college helped buffer Eve from the Pillars of Peril. She maintained sexual purity with her husband and was interested only in cultivating plants, not smoking them. The first two Pillars of Peril—sex and drugs—didn't pose much of a problem for her.

Eve was also well-prepared spiritually for college at Eden. Like her husband, she had a very close relationship with God. And, with like-minded soul mate Adam nearby, getting involved with the wrong friends wasn't an issue.

Although it sounded strange and the consequence seemed severe,

Eve even took to heart the parental admonition Adam's own Father (who, by the way, just happened to be the Founder of the University of Eden) gave him about *what to eat* at Eden. Adam's Father told him that he could eat from *every* tree on the campus of Eden *except* for one in particular.

All in all, college life looked promising for Eve—she was married to the perfect man, attended the perfect school, and was perfectly prepared. By all estimations, she was well on her way to being an Overcomer.

Then one day on campus, Eve crossed paths with the school's most distinguished professor—Professor Serpentine. Now, Professor Serpentine was something to behold for a young student like Eve. He was incredibly intelligent and exceedingly eloquent (not to mention quite handsome). As a matter of fact, Eve felt a little lacking in his presence. Who wouldn't? By all appearances Professor Serpentine knew it all and had it all together.

Surprisingly enough, Professor Serpentine had somehow heard about that odd "tree-eating" admonition Adam's Father had given to him upon entering college and decided to ask Eve about it. The conversation went like this:

> Professor Serpentine: "Did I hear correctly that Adam's Father said you can't eat from every tree on the campus of Eden?"
>
> Eve: "Actually, Adam's Father said we can eat from every tree on campus except for that one over there in the middle, because if we do, we will die."
>
> Professor Serpentine: "*Die* from eating from that tree? You have to be kidding! *Eating from that tree won't cause death.* To the contrary, eating from that tree will make you wiser, more mature, more self-actualized. Do you know why Adam's Father doesn't want you to eat from that tree? Because He's afraid you'll become as wise as He is—and He doesn't want any competition!"
>
> Eve (thinking to herself): "Hmm. I wonder if Professor Serpentine is right about Adam's Father wanting to keep something from us. It does seem like sort of an outdated and unnecessary restriction to me. How could someone so smart, so eloquent, so experienced, so learned as Professor Serpentine be

wrong? I think I'll try it."

And so Eve ate from the one forbidden tree and then gave some of its fruit to Adam and he ate. Unbeknownst to them, in that very moment their University of Instruction turned into their University of Destruction. Almost immediately life spiraled downhill for Adam and Eve—they were expelled from the campus of Eden, endured a difficult life, and true to Adam's Father's word, they eventually died. What had looked so promising ended in disaster. Adam and Eve faced the third Pillar of Peril . . . and stumbled.

"Rock 'n' Roll"—the third Pillar of Peril every student faces in college. It is perhaps the most perilous Pillar of all.

"Wait a second," you say. "Rock 'n' Roll is the third Pillar of Peril?! I have to watch out for a particular type of music in college? I thought we went over that in the last chapter."

The third Pillar of Peril is much more than a genre of music. It is the one thing rock 'n' roll music has represented over the years—*rebellion*. Rebellion against authority and traditional societal norms. Rebellion against "repressive" Judeo-Christian values. Fundamentally, *rebellion against and rejection of God and the Bible.*

Think about the icons of each succeeding generation of rock 'n' roll—from Elvis to the Beatles to the Rolling Stones to Michael Jackson to Madonna to Prince to Britney Spears to Eminem to Usher. What has their music, their lyrics, the lives of these musicians preached, promoted, and paraded? That's right—*rebellion 'n' rejection of God and His Word.*

There is another group of "rock 'n' rollers" who preach rebellion 'n' rejection to young people on an equally great scale to their musical counterparts. Only, these rock 'n' rollers don't sing, *they teach.*

They hold a place of great authority behind the lecterns of higher education across America and the world. They have a captive audience of young people at a most formative and impressionable time of life. They are highly educated and experienced in persuasion and debate. They are esteemed and respected as leaders in their fields. They receive top awards and accolades from their fellow man. They have multiple advanced degrees after their names. They are the elite.

Who are these rock 'n' rollers? *Your professors in college.*

And just like their forefather, Professor Serpentine, they have rebelled against God and rejected His Word. Their dismissal of, or in some cases their disdain for God, Jesus Christ, and the Bible spawns their ideology and fuels their cause—they want to dismantle your Christian faith and replace it with a biblically counterfeit worldview called humanism.

By definition humanism is man's futile and finite attempt to explain the various aspects of the world in which he lives—the origin of the universe, the definition of truth, the basis for morality, the pursuit of religion, the role of family and government, etc.

The important characteristic of humanism to keep in mind is that it emphasizes the flawed wisdom of man and deemphasizes the perfect wisdom of God found in the Bible. Man and his ideas and desires are prioritized in the foreground, while God (if there is such a being) is pushed to the background.

Secular Humanism

At secular (non-religious) colleges the humanism you will encounter promises enlightenment primarily through the avenues of philosophy and science. Your higher education is accomplished through exploring the ideas of prominent thinkers and studying scientific theories of the natural world. God, as presented in the Bible, is left out of the equation.

Religious Humanism

Humanism isn't limited to secular colleges though. At certain Christian colleges the humanism you will face will have a religious spin to it. Religious humanism is the injection of man's flawed ideas, beliefs, and doctrines into the realm of genuine biblical Christianity. In short, it is biblical error caused by human error in interpreting the Bible.

The Battle for Your Mind

The stakes couldn't be bigger—if these humanistic professors are able to win the battle for your mind, you will stray from your Christian faith. Your University of Instruction will turn into your University of Destruction. Guaranteed.

Of course, not *every* college professor is on a mission to tear down your faith, but if you attend a secular university or a liberal Christian college, you are *sure* to run into plenty of them along the way.

Why is this so? Why are so many professors apt to teach humanism, whether secular or religious? Simply answered, once a professor rebels against God and rejects the authority of His Word, he or she is left with nothing but the many and flawed ideologies of man. Cast aside the perfect and what are you left with? Imperfection.

Professor Pharisee

There is also a *genetic* answer as to why so many college professors teach humanism. Let's take a quick look back at the "professors" of Jesus' day. They, too, were the esteemed, the learned, the elite of their time. They were the religious teachers of Israel. Instead of being called professors, though, they were called . . . the *Pharisees*.

While Jesus' words were often characterized by grace and love to those He encountered, this was definitely *not* the case with the Pharisees. His strongest and most derisive rhetoric was reserved for them. Jesus not only never said anything nice about them, He constantly rebuked them.

> Woe to you, scribes and Pharisees, hypocrites! For you are like whitewashed tombs which indeed appear beautiful outwardly, but inside are full of dead men's bones and all uncleanness. Even so you also outwardly appear righteous to men, but inside you are full of hypocrisy and lawlessness. . . . Serpents, brood of vipers! How can you escape the condemnation of hell? Matthew 23:27–28, 33

As you can see, Jesus didn't like the Pharisees.

Jesus clearly understood the negative impact these "professors" were having on their students. He called them "blind leaders of the blind. And if the blind leads the blind, both will fall into a ditch" (Matthew 15:14).

Why did Jesus have so much contempt for the Pharisees? Because they had two attributes He hated—they were *proud* and they were *liars*.

The Pharisees believed they owned the corner on righteousness because they appeared so outwardly "religious." And they thought their high degree of education and intelligence set them above everyone else—they loved their position and power. They were proud.

And rather than teaching justification by faith as the Old Testament and Jesus taught, the Pharisees led many astray by espousing biblical error—that strict adherence to their own made-up list of religious rules gained favor with God (i.e., legalism). This lie not only fueled the Jews' rejection of Jesus as Messiah and His subsequent crucifixion, but just as important, misled countless souls to hell. Whether they realized it or not, they were liars.

As an aside, it is interesting to note that God lists pride and lying at the top of His most hated things:

> These six things the Lord hates, yes, seven are an abomination to Him: *A proud look, a lying tongue,* hands that shed innocent blood, a heart that devises wicked plans, feet that are swift in running to evil, a false witness who speaks lies, and one who sows discord among brethren. Proverbs 6:16–19

So why all the emphasis on the Pharisees and Professor Serpentine? What on earth do they have to do with your professors at college?

Everything. Because they are all of the same lineage . . . they are relatives, if you will.

You see, the motive and method originated by Satan in the Garden of Eden is the same motive and method used by the "professors" (Pharisees) in the time of Christ and the same motive and method used by your modern-day humanistic professors in college.

Their Motive

They're not going to like my saying this, but consciously or unconsciously, the underlying motive of professors who have rebelled against God and rejected His Word is to discredit or derail your Christian faith. They may say they're *tolerant* of all views, but there's one worldview they can't stand—biblical Christianity. As a matter of fact, to their so-called intelligent minds, biblical Christianity is foolishness.

> For *the message of the cross is foolishness to those who are perishing,* but to us who are being saved it is the power of God. . . . For you see your calling, brethren, that *not many wise according to the flesh, not many mighty, not many noble, are called.* But God has chosen the foolish things of the world to put to shame the wise, and God has chosen the weak things of the world to put to shame the things which are mighty . . . that no flesh should glory in His presence. 1 Corinthians 1:18, 26–27, 29

God sees these supposed "wise men" as just the opposite—they are the ones who are fools: "Professing to be wise, they became fools" (Romans 1:22).

Interestingly enough, the word "fool" in the Bible doesn't indicate a lack of intelligence or knowledge (professors certainly have plenty of that). *A fool in the Bible is one who lives his or her life as if there is no God.*

> The fool has said in his heart, "There is no God." They are corrupt, they have done abominable works, there is none who does good. Psalm 14:1

No foolin'—professors who teach a humanistic worldview at odds with the truth of the Bible are the real fools!

Their Method

Not just the motive but the *method* your professors will use is the exact same one used by Satan and the Pharisees—*they will attempt to make you believe a lie.* A lie about God, a lie about the origin of the universe, a lie about morality, a lie about philosophy, a lie about science, a lie about Jesus . . . a lie about anything contrary to the truth of the Bible! Sadly, they don't even realize they are teaching lies because they have hardened their hearts to the truth of God, resulting in spiritual blindness.

Hey, it's not just me coupling the Pharisees and Professor Serpentine together. Jesus said the same thing:

> Why do you not understand My speech? Because you are not able to listen to My word. You are of your father the devil, and the desires of your father you want to do. He was a murderer from the beginning, and does not stand in the truth, because there is no truth in him. When he speaks a lie, he speaks from his own resources, for he is a liar and the father of it. But because I tell you the truth, you do not believe Me. John 8:43–45

Do you see it? There is a Professor Serpentine–inspired lineage of college professors who have rebelled against God, rejected His Word, and have led millions of students into secular or religious humanism. It is indoctrination on a grand scale. They want nothing less than to influence your mind—how you think, how you act, how you view the world.

This is your crossroads: Are you going to cling to God's truth or swallow the professor's lies? Will you battle for truth in the war against error?

First Doubt . . . Then the Lie

The good news is that their game plan is perfectly predictable. Yet they have led so many to destruction through the art of the Lie.

Do you remember the conversation between Professor Serpentine and Eve? Here it is again:

Satan: Has God indeed said, "You shall not eat of every tree of the garden"?

Eve: We may eat the fruit of the trees of the garden; but of the fruit of the tree which is in the midst of the garden, God has said, "You shall not eat it, nor shall you touch it, lest you die."

Satan: You will not surely die. For God knows that in the day you eat of it your eyes will be opened, and you will be like God, knowing good and evil. Genesis 3:1–5

Notice how, instead of starting off with a lie to Eve, Satan completely reversed God's command: "Has God indeed said, 'You shall not eat of every tree of the garden'?"

God actually said, "Of every tree of the garden you may freely eat; but of the tree of the knowledge of good and evil you shall not eat, for in the day that you eat of it you shall surely die" (Genesis 2:16–17).

Do you see the difference? Satan turned the statement in reverse to imply that God was somehow overly demanding and restrictive. He did this to put doubt in Eve's mind about the character of God. To her credit, Eve responded by telling Satan what God's actual command was.

The Lie

Undeterred, Satan then foisted this *blatant lie* upon Eve, the exact opposite of what God said: "You will not surely die. For God knows that in the day you eat of it your eyes will be opened, and you will be like God, knowing good and evil."

Just as you will face in college, Eve had a choice: She could hold fast to what God said or be persuaded by what Satan said. Unfortunately for her, for Adam, for the whole human race, she "opened her mind" to Satan's lie and, true to God's word, suffered the horrible consequences.

Brainwashed!

This, my friend, is the same method your professors will use. Like Satan their father, these godless professors have rebelled 'n' rejected and do not have the truth of God in them. Their very nature is to teach what is contrary to God and His Word. They know, like Satan did with Eve, that if they can get you to think their way, your behavior is sure to follow. Remember what we learned earlier in the book? Your *thoughts* become your *actions* become your *habits* become your *destiny*. They just keep chipping away at a Christian's worldview in the hope of collapsing it.

Someone once said, "If you tell a lie long enough, people will eventually believe it." That is precisely the problem—*the overwhelming majority of students—including Christian students—are unable to discern the humanistic lies they hear from their professors on a daily basis, and slowly they succumb to the indoctrination.*

This is *not* to say you can't learn anything worthwhile from this type of professor, but you do need to be on constant guard for those drops of poison that can pollute your mind.

SECULAR CAMPUS TOUR

Just for kicks, let's poke our heads into a few classrooms around a secular college, pick out the humanistic lies, and contrast them with the truth of God's Word.

Biology 101

Lie: Professor Evolutionist says, "As a result of a cataclysmic explosion, the universe came into existence ten billion years ago. The fossil record then shows that invertebrates made the leap from water to land two million years before humans evolved into their current form."

Truth: "In the beginning God created the heavens and the earth. . . . So God created man in His own image; in the image of God He created him; male and female He created them" (Genesis 1:1, 27).

Values and Ethics 101

Lie: Professor Relativist says, "There is no such thing as absolute truth. What is wrong for you may be right for someone else in the same situation. Who are you to judge someone else? Divisive religious-based concepts of right and wrong only serve to foster guilt and hate rather than tolerance."

Truth: Jesus prayed to His Father and said, "Sanctify them by Your truth. Your word is truth" (John 17:17). "There is a way that seems right to a man, but its end is the way of death" (Proverbs 14:12).

Sociology 101

Lie: Professor Humanist says, "Humans are inherently good. If everyone were given enough education and financial resources, the result would be a united utopian world."

Truth: "There is none righteous, no, not one; there is none who under-stands; there is none who seeks after God. They have all turned aside; they have together become unprofitable; there is none who does good, no, not one" (Romans 3:10–12).

>—•—<

The professors may tell their lies a thousand different ways, but their core message always funnels into these three basic categories:

- The universe evolved (wasn't created by God).
- Truth and morality are relative (not absolute).
- Humans are inherently good (not sinful).

In other words, God (if there is such a being) and the Bible are wrong.

If you believe the lie that you and the universe are the products of random chance and evolution, what degree of purpose and meaning could your life possibly have?

If you believe the lie that truth is relative, on what basis will you make your moral choices?

If you believe the lie that man is inherently good, how do you explain the never-ending cycle of sin in the world—crime, violence, greed, pride, rape, lust, etc.?

It's no wonder people swallow these lies hook, line, and sinker. These professors offer people exactly what their flesh desires—complete personal autonomy without God getting in the way: "I will do whatever I want to do." With this kind of humanistic worldview, you are nothing more than an animal (and will thus behave like one), you (not God) are the master of your ship, and you can do whatever you please (without being accountable to God). "Forget God and His lame ideas—He gets in the way of what I want."

Is it any wonder that many college students live hedonistic, immoral, drunken lives in college?

Of course, there are many variations of these lies you will encounter. Here are just a few:

- "Progressive" political leadership or international unity will solve man's problems.
- Homosexuality is an "orientation" (not a sinful choice), and same-sex marriage is a civil rights struggle.
- Sinful actions like rape, drunkenness, gluttony, drug use, or anti-social behavior are "illnesses" or "diseases" and require medication and more education.
- "Mental disorders" like guilt are best solved by a psychiatrist or psychologist.
- Killing her own unborn or partially born child is a woman's "right."
- There are no differences between men and women and their roles in society.
- Pornography is "art."
- Saving the environment is as important as saving human life.
- Judeo-Christian and non-Judeo-Christian cultures are morally equivalent.
- Christianity is a crutch for weak-minded people.

Lies, lies, lies. For each lie, the Bible offers a contrasting biblical truth.

RELIGIOUS CAMPUS TOUR

Don't think Satan stands outside the door of so-called Christian colleges either. Just like people, *professing* Christian colleges are not necessarily *possessing* Christian colleges. Perhaps even more insidious (because they may be harder to discern), professors at "Christian" colleges that take a liberal, non-literal view of Scripture spread their lies too, in the form of *religious humanism*.

Religious humanism occurs when man inserts or mixes his errant ideas, beliefs, and doctrines into biblical Christianity, thereby changing the meaning and application of Scripture. Because incorrect theology leads to a flawed worldview, this is grave error.

Let's listen in again on a few classes and contrast their lies with the truth of the Bible.

Old Testament Studies 101

Lie: Professor Rationalist says, "Now, these legends and myths in the Bible—the creation account, Noah and the Flood, Moses and the parting of the Red Sea, Jesus' miracles—are meant as symbolic stories to teach principles. Scientists offer no verification that any of these events really happened."

Truth: "The *entirety* of Your word is truth, and every one of Your righteous judgments endures forever" (Psalms 119:160).

New Testament Studies 101

Lie: Professor Skeptic says, "Jesus was a popular teacher in his day, but we have no evidence to suggest that divinity should be ascribed to him."

Truth: Jesus said: "I and My Father are one" (John 10:30). "'Are You then the Son of God?' So [Jesus] said to them, 'You rightly say that I am'" (Luke 22:70).

Religion 101

Lie: Professor Universalist says, "There are many religious roads, but they all lead to God. All sincere people of faith—Christians, Muslims, Hindus, Buddhists, New Age—are on their own distinctive journeys that will conclude at the same glorified place. It's bigoted to believe otherwise."

Truth: Jesus said, "I am the way, the truth, and the life. No one comes to the Father except through Me" (John 14:6). "Nor is there salvation in any other, for there is no other name under heaven given among men by which we must be saved" (Acts 4:12).

These types of professors at "Christian" colleges teach a liberal interpretation of the Bible. They will foist many lies, but again, they all fall into three remarkably similar categories to the ones you will encounter at a secular college . . . except with a "religious" spin:

- The Bible is not the inspired Word of God and source for absolute truth.
- Jesus Christ is not God and the only way to salvation.
- Man is good enough to make the rules for his own religious road.

Now, Satan doesn't care one whit whether you swallow a secular or a religious lie. He's called the "father of religion" for good reason: He originated false religions and biblical liberalism in order to keep you from believing "the (one) way, the (one) truth, and the (one) life" that will save your soul from spending eternity in hell. He will do anything to distract and deceive you from being on that narrow way that leads to life.

Overcoming the Lie

All right, you have received the warning loud and clear that some of your professors, whether at secular or Christian colleges, will be teaching—even encouraging—you to rebel against God and reject His Word through secular or religious humanism. You know that believing any of their lies will change the way you think and thus change the way you live. You have heeded the apostle Paul's warning:

> Beware lest anyone cheat you through philosophy and empty deceit, according to the tradition of men, according to the basic principles of the world, and not according to Christ. Colossians 2:8

Now, the question is this: How are you going to recognize the lies, and what are you going to do about them? *How are you going to battle for the truth in the war against error?*

We could spend from now until doomsday detailing every lie you will hear in college. We could examine every misguided philosopher that you will study, like Freud, Marx, Nietsche, Voltaire, Rousseau, Kant, and Hume. We could scrutinize every godless scientist you will encounter, such as Darwin and Hagel. We could analyze every biblical heresy ever concocted by false teachers and errant theologians. We could study every ideological "ism" known to man:

- Post-modernism (truth is relative to your experience)
- Naturalism (the supernatural, like God and angels, don't exist)
- Atheism (God doesn't exist)
- Deism (an uninvolved higher power exists)
- Marxism (a godless socio-economic political system)
- Nihilism (life is meaningless)
- Pantheism (God and nature are one)

On second thought, I have a better idea. *Know the Truth so you can detect the Lie.*

What did I say? I said, *"Know the Truth so you can detect the Lie."*

Let me explain. Have you ever heard how anti-counterfeiting agents are trained to spot counterfeit money? Do they copiously study every fake bill that's ever been passed? Do they interview the counterfeiters and find out their secrets?

While they might do some of this, what they primarily focus on is studying the *real thing* . . . over and over and over! When they are so familiar with real currency, they can spot counterfeit currency in a heart-beat.

Do you get the point? *When you intimately know the truth of the Bible, you will be able to detect the counterfeit lies coming your way in college.* It is as simple as that. To counteract the brainwash you will receive in class, you need to have your mind continually cleansed with the truth of the Word of God . . . every day. It truly is the *only* antidote to their destructive lies.

Sound too simple? Don't know where to start in your Bible? Don't understand what it means? Too boring? Fret no more—you will find out how to read, study, and use your Bible in the next chapter when we devise your collegiate game plan for victory.

The Lie Sounds Good

Now, there is nothing wrong with learning about the philosophies, scientific theories, and errant theologies that have misguided millions over the years. If you're strong enough in your beliefs and familiar with your Bible, it can actually strengthen your faith. Be careful, though; much of what you will hear from your professors about the philosophies, scientific theories, apostasies, and -isms *will sound intelligent, reasonable, and even true.* You wouldn't believe the Lie otherwise.

And in the course of spinning their lies, they'll make biblical Christianity sound dumb, a crutch for simple-minded mental midgets. They'll say the Bible has many errors and discrepancies. They'll say it is full of hate and bigotry. They'll say it is not relevant for today.

Possessors know better: There is only one Being (God) and one Book (the Bible) that is fully trustworthy, without error, and sufficient for life. That is the decision you will have to make: On what am I going to base my life and daily decisions—the Word of God or the mind of man?

To help you make the right choice, consider that all the philosophers and their philosophies, all the apostate theologians and their errant theologies have come and gone with history (not to mention the professors who have taught them), but one thing hasn't changed:

> Jesus Christ is the same yesterday, today, and forever. Hebrews 13:8
> [Jesus said,] "Heaven and earth will pass away, but My words will by no means pass away." Matthew 24:35

Now, there's a foundation you can trust!

What to do? What to do? There you are sitting in class one day when your professor says, "Don't be so simplistic as to think that the Judeo-Christian values of America's founders haven't had a long-standing, negative effect on this country. They brought us the oppression of minorities and women, intolerance for other religions, and an imperialistic foreign policy. Thank God we've made so much progress, no thanks to those religious right-wing extremists who would take us back to a time of repression and intolerance."

While the rest of the sheep in your class are nodding approvingly, thinking the professor is oh so brilliant, you detect that his statement is false. There may have been some injustice in our nation's history, but not as a result of our Judeo-Christian values (biblical values). You have a choice.

Will You Conform, Conceal, or Confront?

You can *conform* to the professor's lie like most of the class is going to do and go around like a dutiful *rebel-ette* parroting your professor. Or you can *conceal* your opposing beliefs and keep quiet. Or you can *confront* your professor now or after class.

What do you do? Obviously not conform. If you aren't able to proclaim and defend your opposing view, it may be better to conceal. If you decide to confront, do it in a most respectful manner—perhaps one-on-one with your professor after class.

Recognize and Replace

And do it like Christ. When tempted by Satan, Jesus *recognized* his lies and *replaced* them with the truth of Scripture (Matthew 4). Satan confronted Christ with three falsehoods, and three times Jesus responded, "It is written . . ." and then went on to quote a verse of Scripture. Don't put yourself in the position of defending your own words; let the Word of God speak for itself.

You might respond to your professor this way:

> The Bible doesn't teach oppression toward women and minorities, imperialism, and intolerance for other religions. To the contrary, the Bible says that women and minorities should be loved, not repressed. For example, *it is written,* "Husbands, love your wives, just as Christ also loved the church and gave Himself for her" (Ephesians 5:25). Jesus also said, "Blessed are the merciful, for they shall obtain mercy" (Matthew 5:7).
>
> The Bible also encourages peace amongst the nations: "Blessed are the peacemakers, for they shall be called sons of God" (Matthew 5:9).
>
> And as for intolerance of other religions, Christianity is open to everyone. It is written in John 3:16–17: "For God so loved the world that He gave His only begotten Son, that whoever believes in Him should not perish but have everlasting life. For God did not send His Son into the world to condemn the world, but that the world through Him might be saved."

And then get ready! You may be mocked, shamed, ridiculed, persecuted, and embarrassed by your professor and classmates—you might even be given a lower grade. This is the potential result for holding up the banner of Christ . . . but there is a blessing for those who do:

> Blessed are you when they revile and persecute you, and say

all kinds of evil against you falsely for My sake. Rejoice and be exceedingly glad, for great is your reward in heaven, for so they persecuted the prophets who were before you. Matthew 5:11–12

Two Types of Wisdom

The third Pillar of Peril can be aptly summed up as a battle between two different kinds of wisdom: the wisdom of the *world* versus the wisdom of the *Word*. One's source is the mind of man, the other's source is the mind of God as written in the Bible. God's wisdom is always true. Man's wisdom is always flawed.

Professors who have rebelled against God and rejected His Word teach the wisdom of the *world* at odds with the Bible. This wisdom comes from increasing one's knowledge of the universe and assimilating humanistic philosophies like evolution, moral relativism, and the goodness of man.

In their never-ending search for truth (which, ironically enough, they don't even think exists!), they like to borrow the words of Jesus: "And you shall know the truth, and the truth shall make you free" (John 8:32). Of course, they fail to understand that Jesus was referring to himself as the source of all truth, not the philosophies of man.

On the other hand, the wisdom of the *Word* has nothing to do with human intelligence—it is available to all Possessors of the indwelling Holy Spirit. Godly wisdom starts with knowing that God is the Creator, Sustainer, and Judge of mankind and that He has defined His will and ways in the Bible. A person with this wisdom is able to skillfully apply the Word of God to everyday life.

Godly wisdom leads to inner peace and assurance for the future. Worldly wisdom leads to sin, confusion, and despair. The conversation between Jesus and Pontius Pilate illustrates this well:

> [Jesus said,] "For this cause I was born, and for this cause I have come into the world, that I should bear witness to the truth. Everyone who is of the truth hears My voice." Pilate said to Him, "What is truth?" John 18:37–38

Jesus was the embodiment of truth. Pilate had been affected by the humanism of his day and, like modern-day professors, didn't even think truth existed. He had believed the Lie.

Overcomers, don't believe the Lie. Decide the Bible is going to be your basis for truth. Read it as your daily spiritual food. Recognize the Lie—whether secular or religious humanism—when it comes your way. Replace it with the truth of the Word.

For when you do, victory over the third Pillar of Peril will be yours.

VERY IMPORTANT PRINCIPLE:

The third Pillar of Peril is a battle for your mind. Will you believe God and His Word or your professors and their secular or religious humanism?

MESSAGE TO MEMORIZE:

For the message of the cross is foolishness to those who are perishing, but to us who are being saved it is the power of God. For it is written: "I will destroy the wisdom of the wise, and bring to nothing the understanding of the prudent." Where is the wise? Where is the scribe? Where is the disputer of this age? Has not God made foolish the wisdom of this world? 1 CORINTHIANS 1:18–20

PERSONAL COMMITMENT:

I will learn the wisdom of the Word so that I can recognize the lies of the world and replace them with the truth of Scripture.

Signature:

Date:

10. THE GAME PLAN

Get ready to be an Overcomer!

The game plan. No successful person, student, athlete, team, corporation, or military operates without a well-thought-out and detailed game plan. And that is precisely what you will discover in this chapter—a practical game plan for victory over the three Pillars of Peril on campus.

You won't get trite theories, ponderous platitudes, or gross generalizations. As a matter of fact, you're not even going to get a Plan B just in case Plan A fails. Tried and tested over the ages, Plan A works every time because the perfect Coach drew it up and detailed it in His perfect game plan Book.

The good news for you is that your college game plan is not complicated, but rather is all about the *fundamentals*. Why the fundamentals? Because executing the fundamentals under pressure is what separates the best from the rest—successful people in every field of work know and practice this.

For example, a basketball player has to be able to make the most basic shot—the free throw—at the end of the game. A car mechanic must completely grasp the basic principles of ignition and combustion before repairing an engine. A surgeon must understand the basics of hygiene and anatomy before doing a complex surgery. If the fundamentals aren't sound, the end result will be a poor one.

So what are the fundamentals of your college game plan? What fundamentals do you need to be an Overcomer on campus?

Think GPA

No, not your Grade Point Average (although it's nice to have a good one!). The GPA I'm talking about is a spiritual one, and it measures how successfully you interact with **G**od, your **P**eers, and your **A**uthorities. These are the fundamentals of your college game plan. How well you interact with each one of these will determine your degree of success on campus . . . and in life, for that matter.

Sounds pretty easy, but the reality is that most college students have a very low spiritual GPA. They have little or no interaction with God, they have the wrong kind of interaction with their peers, and they resist interaction with their authorities. All of which explains why so many students become shipwrecked in college. They don't know, don't care to know, and thus can't execute these *fundamentals*.

Not so for the Overcomer. The Overcomer has a high spiritual GPA. Let's rate how well he or she executes the fundamentals on a four-point scale.

The Overcomer has close interaction with God on a regular basis (3.5), interacts with his peers in a mutually beneficial way (3.5), and derives full benefit from interaction with his authorities (3.5). Yes, the Overcomer excels at the fundamentals of Christian living—interaction with God, his peers, and his authorities—and fully reaps the benefit of a successful college experience. He has a 3.5 GPA and still has room for improvement!

When Jesus was a young person, the Bible says this about His spiritual GPA:

> Then He went down with [His parents] and came to Nazareth, and was subject to them, but His mother kept all these things in her heart. And Jesus increased in wisdom and stature, and in favor with God and men. Luke 2:51–52

Do you see it? Jesus was subject to His parents' authority and was in favor with God and His peers. He interacted well (actually, perfectly) with God, His peers, and His authorities. The perfect Young Person gave the perfect example of mastering the fundamentals of Christian living. But of course—Jesus had a 4.0 spiritual GPA!

The D-word

You too can excel at these fundamentals. But it does take one quality of character that many people lack. It takes one attribute from which most of us shy away. It requires one trait that cannot be avoided. Can you guess what it is?

Discipline. The dreaded D-word. The dictionary defines it this way: "Training intended to produce a specified character or pattern of behavior." It's interesting that the word *training* is used. Do you know what the training of top athletes is like? It is hard work, it occurs regularly, it takes perseverance.

I would imagine that you are aware of these fundamentals. *Knowing* them probably isn't the issue, but *doing* them might be! It takes plenty of personal discipline to excel at these fundamentals. No one can do it for you. It doesn't happen by osmosis. There are no shortcuts. You must put in the necessary time and effort to have a high spiritual GPA.

I wish I could tell you it's easy. In this fast-food culture in which we live, everything has to be instantaneous or it's unpopular and deemed not worth the wait or the effort. Lunch has to be ready in three minutes, email or cell phone communication requires immediate response, and a sermon shouldn't be longer than twenty minutes or people will tune out. We want it, and we want it now!

Yet this is not the way God operates. Notice the way the apostle Paul exhorted his understudy, Timothy, to be diligent and disciplined in His interaction with God.

> Be diligent to present yourself approved to God, a worker who does not need to be ashamed, rightly dividing the word of truth. 2 Timothy 2:15

In other words, it takes day-by-day diligence to increase your spiritual GPA. It's the same for improving your academic GPA, right? And by the way, there isn't necessarily a correlation between your academic GPA and your spiritual GPA. Oftentimes those with a high academic GPA have a very low spiritual GPA and vice versa. The difference comes down to growing in the wisdom of the Word rather than in the wisdom of the world. Human intelligence is a noble pursuit, but without godly wisdom, it is a vain pursuit.

The reason I'm telling you that focusing on the fundamentals takes discipline is that I want you to be prepared. Sometimes when we think a test, an athletic contest, or anything in life is going to be easy, and then it turns out to be hard, we stumble and fall because we aren't prepared for it. But like anything worthwhile in life—and there is nothing *more* worthwhile than excelling at these fundamentals—personal discipline is required to attain it.

Now, I don't want to intimidate you either. Remember, if you're a Possessor, you possess the indwelling Holy Spirit, who gives you the power, the motivation, the *discipline* to succeed. As a matter of fact, God promises to give you the desire and power to excel at these fundamentals. Just make yourself available. He'll do the rest.

> For it is God who works in you both to will and to do for His good pleasure. Philippians 2:13

So what makes up your successful college game plan? Excelling at the fundamentals—interaction with God, your peers, your authorities—and personal discipline on your part to make it happen.

Now, let's go after that high spiritual GPA!

The College Marathon

Is there a sport more basic than long-distance running? I mean, all you do is . . . run! Very little equipment is necessary, there are not a lot of rules, and there isn't too much technical know-how. Just put one foot in front of the other, do it for a long time, and cross the finish line.

Earlier in the book we compared college to a marathon race. There's a starting point (first day), an ending point (graduation day), and a long road in between (four years). Let's resurrect the marathon analogy for purposes of your college game plan.

So there you are, getting ready for the big "race" that starts around September 1. So what do you do—show up on September 1, drop your bags on your dorm room floor, and say, "Let's go?" You do if you're in shape, if you know the course, if you have your game plan down pat.

But if you're not prepared for the race, if you haven't trained yourself into top shape, if you have no idea what the course is like, if you have no game plan . . . well, you're hurtin' for certain! And the bad news is the race is going to start on September 1 whether you're ready or not. Guaranteed, you're going to be fading after a couple of miles, wandering off course, and struggling just to keep up. There's nothing you can do about it now, though; you're going to have to figure it out as you go and play catch-up.

Therefore, if at all possible, you need to start working on the fundamentals before you go to college.

That's right, get in shape before the race! Now, you may be reading this book and are already in college . . . already running the race, if you will. No problem. It ain't over. You just start right now working on your spiritual GPA, and before you know it you'll be fit and running strong. But if you are reading this before entering college, this is your big chance to start off on the right foot.

Enough of the pep talk. Let's get started on improving each fundamental of your game plan—interaction with God, interaction with your peers, interaction with your authorities—so that you can successfully execute your game plan for victory on campus.

Let's get started raising your spiritual GPA!

VERY IMPORTANT PRINCIPLE:

Your game plan for victory on campus requires that you diligently improve and successfully execute the three fundamentals of a high spiritual GPA—interaction with God, interaction with your peers, interaction with your authorities.

MESSAGE TO MEMORIZE:

Be diligent to present yourself approved to God, a worker who does not need to be ashamed, rightly dividing the word of truth. 2 TIMOTHY 2:15

GAME PLAN FUNDAMENTAL ONE: INTERACTION WITH GOD

It's all about *relating* and *renewing.*

What does the first fundamental of your game plan—*interaction with God*—involve? It involves deepening your *relationship* with God so that your mind and spirit can be *renewed.*

God created you to have a relationship with Him, to fellowship with Him. He wants to communicate with you on a daily basis. He wants you to know His nature and character. He wants your character transformed to be more like His Son, Jesus Christ, so that you can be an Overcomer just as He was.

When you interact with God, you are transformed through the "renewing of your mind."

> And do not be conformed to this world, but be transformed by the renewing of your mind, that you may prove what is that good and acceptable and perfect will of God. Romans 12:2

A "renewed" mind is one that has been restored, refreshed, or revitalized from the negative influence of the world and your flesh. As a car gets dirty when you drive it, so your mind gets sullied just by living in this fallen world—we all are continually being influenced by the world, often imperceptibly. Just as a car needs a regular car wash, so your mind needs a daily *brainwash!*

A renewed mind is so important because it gives you the ability to recognize the lies and temptations you will face on campus and to replace them with the truth of the Word. In other words, a renewed mind allows you to know the will of God so that you can be an Overcomer.

Relating

So practically, how do you deepen your interaction with God so that you will have a renewed mind? Well, how do you deepen your relationship with another person—a girlfriend, a boyfriend, anyone? You spend quality time with them!

It is no different with God. You need to spend quality time with Him too . . . *every day.*

Think about it. If you had a childhood friend whom you never see or talk to anymore, you will obviously not be as close to that person as you once were. A relationship can't function without interaction. To rekindle the relationship and keep it going, it would take spending time together and communicating on a regular basis.

Many Christians, not just high school and college students, say that God feels "distant." The obvious response is, "Well, how often do you seek Him out for fellowship?" *"Oh, a couple times a month."* How close can you be to someone when you communicate only twice a month? You probably wouldn't go a day without calling or emailing your best friend three times! It is no wonder you are so close to him or her.

The Bible makes this point very clear and simple:

Draw near to God and He will draw near to you. James 4:8a

- God draws near to you through His written Word. He just waits patiently for you to draw near to Him by reading it.
- God draws near to you through His indwelling Holy Spirit reminding you to obey His Word. He just waits patiently for you to draw near to Him in prayer.

This is precisely how interacting with God works. God talks to you through His Word. We talk to God through prayer. The Holy Spirit stands in the middle to clarify God's Word and help us pray back to God. It's as simple as that.

This is *not* normal communication though. No, it's not magical or mystical. It's better than that—it's *supernatural*.

The Bible

For instance, take God's personal letter to you—the Bible. It is a unique book. As a matter of fact, it is completely different from any other book ever written. In chapter nine, on the third Pillar of Peril, we discovered the Bible's claim to be the final and absolute truth. Yet, it has many other qualities too—supernatural ones. Here are just two:

- The Bible is inspired by God.

   All Scripture is given by inspiration of God, and is profitable for doctrine, for reproof, for correction, for instruction in righteousness, that the man of God may be complete, thoroughly equipped for every good work. 2 Timothy 3:16–17

- The Bible is living and powerful.

> For the word of God is living and powerful, and sharper than any two-edged sword, piercing even to the division of soul and spirit, and of joints and marrow, and is a discerner of the thoughts and intents of the heart. Hebrews 4:12

Do you know of any other book that God claims to have inspired, that is living and powerful, and that can change your earthly life and eternal destiny? Didn't think so.

This is why I can't emphasize enough the truthfulness, the relevancy, the sufficiency, the inerrancy, the power of the Bible. Every other book, scholar, teacher, philosopher, scientist, and professor pales in comparison. The Bible is your greatest resource!

For the Overcomer, the Bible is his or her primary weapon for fighting the spiritual battles on campus. Think about it: God has actually made it *easy* for you—your resource for victory is all in one Book! As your mind and spirit are renewed daily with Scripture, you will be able to *recognize* the lies and temptations on campus and *replace* them with the truth of the Word. This is the Overcomer's secret to success.

Prayer

Now, what about *your* communication to God—prayer? It is unique and, once again, supernatural. You can speak to God out loud or in your thoughts, and He hears you. But it gets even better—He answers according to His will!

> Now this is the confidence that we have in Him, that if we ask anything according to His will, He hears us. And if we know that He hears us, whatever we ask, we know that we have the petitions that we have asked of Him. 1 John 5:14–15

The Holy Spirit

Finally, the Holy Spirit's intermediary role between you and God is also supernatural. He indwells you upon salvation and works as God's personal representative to you. He reminds you to obey God's Word and touches your conscience when you sin. He facilitates God's communication to you by clarifying what the Bible means and how it is to be applied. He also facilitates your communication back to God by helping you pray according to God's will.

- The Holy Spirit clarifies God's communication to us.

  But the Helper, the Holy Spirit, whom the Father will send in My name, He will teach you all things, and bring to your remembrance all things that I said to you. John 14:26

- The Holy Spirit helps us communicate back to God in prayer.

  Likewise the Spirit also helps in our weaknesses. For we do not know what we should pray for as we ought, but the Spirit Himself makes intercession for us with groanings which cannot be uttered. Romans 8:26

The Commitment

Now you understand how interaction with God works—through the Word, through prayer, and through the Holy Spirit. What do you need to do to excel at this first fundamental of your game plan?

Only one thing: *Make a commitment to interact with God daily.*

The following is *not* an overstatement: *After your decision to follow Jesus Christ, a commitment to interact with God on a daily basis is the most important commitment you will make in life.*

More important than a commitment to moral purity? More important than a commitment to avoiding drugs and alcohol? Absolutely, because it's unlikely you'll be able to keep those commitments if you're not interacting with God on a regular basis. This is the commitment that makes all the others happen. This is your spiritual base of operations.

The Latin phrase *sine qua non* describes the importance of interacting with God. It means, "Without which there is nothing." In other words, if you don't interact with God, you have nothing spiritually. Show me a Christian who doesn't interact with God regularly, and I'll show you a weak or backslidden or stumbling Christian. Your interaction with God is your daily source of strength, guidance, and growth. Interacting with God is indispensable to your Christian faith.

Now Interact!

What does interacting with God entail? It means that you spend some time every day communicating with Him through reading His Word and praying. It means *disciplining* yourself (there's the D-word again!) to set aside that time every day.

Pray...

Start out your time with God by praying to Him for a few minutes. It doesn't need to be long or fancy—just talk to him out loud or in your thoughts.

Jesus set the example for how to do it:

> In this manner, therefore, pray: Our Father in heaven, hallowed be Your name. Your kingdom come. Your will be done on earth as it is in heaven. Give us this day our daily bread. And forgive us our debts, as we forgive our debtors. And do not lead us into temptation, but deliver us from the evil one. For Yours is the kingdom and the power and the glory forever. Amen. Matthew 6:9–13

Do you see the different aspects of Jesus' prayer? The acronym ACTS teaches us how to pray:

- **A**dore or praise God for His many and perfect attributes—His holiness, perfection, mercy, justice, love, and grace.
- **C**onfess any sin in your life to God. Sin breaks our fellowship with God, and confessing it wipes the slate clean. As a Christian, claim the forgiveness that God has already given you when Christ satisfied God's wrath for your sin—past, present, and future—on the cross.
- **T**hank God for everything—the blessings in life and even the trials.
- **S**upplicate or ask God for various needs in your life, all according "to His will." Ask God for the Holy Spirit's leading as you begin to read His Word.

...Then Read

After praying, continue your interaction with God by reading carefully a chapter of Scripture. What should you read? The Bible is actually sixty-six books rolled into one large book. There is no need to be intimidated by the size of the Bible. It breaks down easily into distinct sections.

The thirty-nine books of the *Old Testament* can be divided into three categories:

- Genesis through Esther: the creation of the world and the history of Israel
- Job through Song of Solomon: poetry, songs, and wisdom
- Isaiah through Malachi: the Prophets and their prophecies

The twenty-seven books of the New Testament can also be divided into three categories:

- the Gospels (Matthew, Mark, Luke, John): biographies of Jesus Christ
- Acts and the Epistles: Christian living and the beginnings of the church
- Revelation: future prophecy and judgment

So where should you start? How about reading just one chapter a day to get into a routine and gain momentum?

Proverbs: There are thirty-one chapters in this book of wisdom; read one a day for the first month.

Gospel of John: Get to know Jesus Christ better in this New Testament biography. A chapter a day will take the next twenty-one days.

Genesis: Find out how God created the universe and man. Read fascinating and true stories about the great flood, Abraham and Isaac, and the nation of Israel in Egypt. A chapter a day will take you the next fifty days.

Romans: Learn the great doctrines of the Christian faith as written by Paul in his letter to the Romans. Read this one slowly, as there's a lot in it. A chapter a day will take you sixteen days.

Exodus: Jump back to the Old Testament to find out how God miraculously brought the nation of Israel to the Promised Land. A chapter a day will take you through the next forty days.

Galatians, Ephesians, Philippians, Colossians: Read Paul's letters to upstart churches in these cities. Twenty total chapters will take you twenty days.

And while you're reading through these books, tack on one chapter a day from the book of *Psalms*. The songbook of the Bible has 150 (mainly short) chapters in it, so you'll finish Psalms almost concurrently with the rest of your reading.

All right, you get the picture. I just gave you a chapter a day program that will take you 177 days to finish. That's almost half a year! And we haven't even scratched the surface—the sequence I have suggested is just to get you started. There's plenty more to read, study, and learn in the Bible from both the Old and New Testaments. It's the Book for a lifetime.

If a certain book doesn't interest you right now, no problem—move on to another one. There's nothing wrong with that. You don't have to read the Bible from start to finish. But whatever you read, read it not just for knowledge but to understand the character of God so that you can become more like His Son, Jesus Christ, the central Person and theme of the entire Bible.

Say What?

Don't understand what the Bible is saying? By all means buy a study Bible with footnotes so you can check out the meaning of any given passage. I personally like the *MacArthur Study Bible* by pastor/teacher John MacArthur. Or try reading a different translation of the Bible (I prefer the New King James Version or the New American Standard Bible). Better yet, ask your parents to buy it for you. I promise you, they won't say no to this one!

Extra Credit

How about some extra credit? Write down a few personal notes on the passage you read—perhaps how you can apply it to your life. While you're at it, keep a prayer list so that your faith can be strengthened as you see how God answers your prayers.

Passage in Your Pocket

Finally, carry a "passage in your pocket." What does that mean? It means to find a passage of Scripture to memorize—perhaps a verse or two or maybe a whole chapter. Choose one that deals with a personal struggle you're having or one that reminds you of the greatness of God and His Word. Start out by writing down one verse on a note card or in your PDA and carry it in your pocket throughout the day. Pull it out, read it, memorize it, and then refer to it later. Before you can say like

Jesus, "It is written . . ." you have to know in your mind what actually *is written*.

Memorization of Scripture leads to "meditation" on Scripture, which is thinking about, chewing over, reflecting on the Word of God on a regular basis. Want to start thinking like God? Want to have some of His wisdom? Start memorizing and then meditating on Scripture—it is the most powerful way to overcome temptation and live a victorious Christian life. "Hiding the Word in your heart" is the secret to spiritual success.

> Your word I have hidden in my heart, that I might not sin against You. Psalm 119:11
>
> Blessed is the man who walks not in the counsel of the ungodly, nor stands in the path of sinners, nor sits in the seat of the scornful; but his delight is in the law of the Lord, and in His law he *meditates* day and night. He shall be like a tree planted by the rivers of water, that brings forth its fruit in its season, whose leaf also shall not wither; and whatever he does shall prosper. Psalm 1:1–3

E-Pastor

There is one more excellent way you can interact with God on campus. In addition to reading the Word yourself, *hear* the Word taught electronically by a pastor on the radio, Internet, or television. Tune into your local Christian radio station and find a sound teacher of the Bible. Listen on your headset while you walk to class, work out in the gym, or spend time in your room.

Or listen on the Internet. The Web site *www.oneplace.com* has dozens of pastors and Bible teachers. Find a biblically sound one, like John MacArthur, Alistair Begg, D. James Kennedy, Michael Youssef, or my pastor, Leith Anderson, and listen online or download the message to your MP3 player.

The Bible says this about *hearing* the Word:

> And how shall they believe in Him of whom they have not heard? And how shall they hear without a preacher? And how shall they preach unless they are sent? As it is written: "How beautiful are the feet of those who preach the gospel of peace, who bring glad tidings of good things!" . . . *So then faith comes*

by hearing, and hearing by the word of God. Romans 10:14–15, 17

While none of these should be a substitute for attending church, there are plenty of ways for you to interact with God on campus through reading—and hearing—the Word!

FAQs

And now to answer some of those frequently asked questions:

1. Why do I have to read the Bible every day? I'll answer this question with two questions for you. Why do you eat every day? Or why do you bathe every day? If you don't eat every day, you will get very weak and even lose your appetite in time. It's the same thing with your "spiritual food"—if you don't take in spiritual food every day, you'll become weak spiritually and eventually lose your spiritual appetite to interact with God. It's the same without your daily "spiritual shower"—you'll start to stink in your Christian life!

Another reason to interact with God every day is that we all have extremely short memories and need to be reminded of God's attributes, our weaknesses, what His will is, and how we can please Him. Like a hungry lion, Satan roams about looking for that emaciated, susceptible Christian who doesn't interact with God. Your interaction with God is like putting on spiritual armor to defend yourself for that day:

> Put on the whole armor of God, that you may be able to stand against the wiles of the devil. For we do not wrestle against flesh and blood, but against principalities, against powers, against the rulers of the darkness of this age, against spiritual hosts of wickedness in the heavenly places. Ephesians 6:11–12

2. What if I don't feel like interacting with God or the Bible seems dry or I'm not getting anything out of the time? In the words of a well-known athletic shoe manufacturer: "Just do it!" Never listen to your negative feelings when it comes to interacting with God. Like a marathon runner, there are going to be days you feel like training, days you don't, and everything in between.

Believe me: You will always get something out of your interaction with God. Remember how we discussed the supernatural nature of the Bible? The Bible always has an effect on you, *always* has an impact. It is always worthwhile to read God's Word. It never returns void:

So shall My word be that goes forth from My mouth; it shall not return to Me void, but it shall accomplish what I please, and it shall prosper in the thing for which I sent it. Isaiah 55:11

As the saying goes, "The Word keeps you from sin, and sin keeps you from the Word." That's good enough reason right there to read it even when you don't feel like it.

3. *What if I don't have time?* Bad excuse. Most people are awake for at least fifteen hours a day. Every person, and I mean *every* person, can set aside fifteen *minutes* for the most important thing of the day—interacting with God. Think of the time you spend surfing the Internet, watching television, talking on the phone, eating meals, studying, or hanging out with your friends. It's just a matter of carving out fifteen minutes every day and keeping that time sacred.

By the way, any time of day is fine; just so you do it. I highly recommend interacting with God right after you wake up in the morning. It gets your mind and spirit ready for the day. Nothing unexpected gets in the way, and if it does, you can get back to reading it later in the day. Leave the Bible right next to your bed. If you miss a morning, place the Bible on your pillow so you'll remember to interact with God before going to bed that night. Whatever you do, don't miss *one* day! That is your commitment to interact with God.

4. *Are there answers to the unanswerables?* As you read the Bible, there are going to be plenty of issues you don't understand. Join the club—there are some issues in the Bible that *no one* understands! You will come across several of the deep questions of life that Bible scholars have been debating for centuries, such as these:

- How can a loving God allow so much suffering in the world?
- Why did God create man with the capacity to sin?
- Why are some people saved and not others?

Let me give you two answers to these *unanswerables*.

The first is that we humans have limited minds and understanding. Our minds are downright finite, unlike God, who is all-knowing and infinite. There are some things in the Bible that are just beyond our human minds. This verse explains that:

"For My thoughts are not your thoughts, nor are your ways

My ways," says the Lord. "For as the heavens are higher than the earth, so are My ways higher than your ways, and My thoughts than your thoughts." Isaiah 55:8–9

The second answer is that God has chosen to keep some things a mystery for now. Why? Because He's God and that's His prerogative. Period. End of story.

Everything isn't perfectly clear now, but it will be someday when we join Him in heaven.

> For now we see in a mirror, dimly, but then face to face. Now I know in part, but then I shall know just as I also am known. 1 Corinthians 13:12

In the meantime, have faith in the sovereignty of God—He's all-knowing, all-powerful, perfectly just, holy, and wise. He knows exactly what He's doing. Don't let the mysteries, the unanswerable questions, depress your faith. God has revealed all that we need to know for right now. Trust Him—He's God!

A Renewed Mind

Reading the Bible. Praying. Listening to the indwelling Holy Spirit. Meditating on Scripture. Hearing the Word taught.

This is how you interact with God daily. This is how you are transformed by the renewing of your mind.

- You will escape sexual temptation by remembering, "Flee sexual immorality . . ."
- You will avoid drugs and alcohol by recalling, "Be not drunk . . . but be filled with the Spirit."
- You will recognize the lies of your humanistic professors and replace them with "The Bible is the truth and it says . . ."

Your daily interaction with God is the first fundamental of your game plan for victory on campus, the cornerstone of a high spiritual GPA. With your inner battle between the Spirit and your flesh, the pressure to conform on campus, and the assault of the three Pillars of Peril, it is absolutely necessary that you renew your mind every day by interacting with God.

Think of your daily interaction with God as recharging your spiritual battery. Better yet, consider it the greatest of privileges to personally communicate with God himself! Through reading the Word and praying, with the Holy Spirit as your guide, you have powerful resources for recognizing the lies and temptations you will face on campus and for replacing them with the truth of Scripture.

Make your commitment right now to interact with God—discipline yourself. You've thought about it—now take action and it will soon become a habit. Don't let anything get in the way of your top daily priority.

This is how you avoid the University of Destruction. This is how you become an Overcomer on campus!

VERY IMPORTANT PRINCIPLE:

Your commitment to interact with God on a daily basis will transform you by renewing your mind so that you can overcome the spiritual obstacles on campus.

MESSAGE TO MEMORIZE:

And do not be conformed to this world, but be transformed by the renewing of your mind, that you may prove what is that good and acceptable and perfect will of God.
ROMANS 12:2

PERSONAL COMMITMENT:

I commit to interacting with God every day in college.

Signature:

Date:

GAME PLAN FUNDAMENTAL TWO: INTERACTION WITH YOUR PEERS

Think you have a grasp of the first fundamental? Then let's move on to fundamental number two of your game plan—interaction with your peers.

Let me say this right off the bat: *Your friendships in college will make or break you.*

One verse perfectly summarizes the "make or break" power of peers:

> He who walks with wise men will be wise, but the companion of fools will be destroyed. Proverbs 13:20

Read it again. Memorize it. Take it to heart.

The fact is this: *You become like the people you're with.*

This is a simple "cause and effect" principle—one of those "if/then" statements. *If* you do this, *then* this will be the result.

If your friends are Overcomers, *then* you will become more like them. *If* your friends are Compromisers or Pretenders, *then* you'll become more like them.

I'm positive I'm telling you something you already know. Everyone has been warned of the perils of spending time with the wrong friends. Undoubtedly, you have seen the result when someone you know starts hanging out with a questionable crowd. Before long that person takes on the characteristics of the group in speech, actions, and even dress. The apostle Paul wrote this:

> Do not be deceived: Evil company corrupts good habits. 1 Corinthians 15:33

Perhaps you've experienced this in your own life. Think about some of your current friends. You probably have a friend or two who is always trying to get you to do something that makes you feel a little uncomfortable. They ask you to go to worthless movies, they talk about sex and drinking, they want to go out partying all the time. They're always trying to get away with something, and you feel the pressure to either go along or resist.

On the other hand, you probably have another friend with whom you don't always need to put up your guard. This friend does not pull you down but rather gravitates toward activities and conversations that aren't sinful. As a matter of fact, this friend may even encourage your spiritual growth—he or she talks about God, wants to go to Christian events, and desires to live a holy life.

The first type of friend is *detrimental* to you; the second is *beneficial*. There's your goal for interacting with your peers: *mutually beneficial friendships*. You choose friends who make you stronger as a person, and in return you make them stronger too.

Levels of Friendship

Before we go any further, have you ever thought about how many different *types* of friendships you have? On one end of the spectrum, you probably have a few core friends with whom you spend most of your time and in whom you'd confide almost anything. On the other end of the spectrum, you have many acquaintances with whom you spend less time and in whom you'd confide almost nothing. And then there are some friends in between who aren't too close but not too distant either.

And just like your interaction with God, the level of friendship and its impact on you—positive or negative—is dependent on the amount of personal time and communication you invest in each other. In other words, acquaintances have much less of an impact on you than your close friends. Makes sense, right?

Discernment

The critical part of interacting with your peers is discerning the true character of your existing friends and any other prospective friends.

Why is this discernment (i.e., spiritual perception) so critical? *Because friendships need to be regulated.* Regulating your friendships means purposely drawing near to the right kind of friends and keeping a safe distance from the wrong kind of friends. As you know, friendships can form, grow, or dissolve in a hurry, and as the level of friendship changes, so does the potential impact on you.

You can't be *passive* when it comes to friendships. You must learn how to *recognize* what type of person someone is and then *regulate* the friendship accordingly. Potentially detrimental friendships must be kept at arm's length—less time and communication together. Potentially beneficial friendships should be pursued—more time and communication together.

The fact is that most people have very little discernment and just sort of fall into friendships. To thrive in college, though, you must know how to *purposely* choose to spend time in mutually beneficial friendships. You must search for them as you would for hidden treasure:

> True friends are like diamonds, precious and rare; fake friends are like autumn leaves, found everywhere. Author Unknown

Equally Yoked

For the Possessor mutually beneficial friendships can occur *only* with another Possessor. This is why the Bible commands Christians not to be "unequally yoked" with unbelievers or with believers who are habitually practicing sin. A shared love for God and obedience to Him creates an "equal yoke" between two Possessors. Since they are the same "animal" (i.e., same nature), they can help pull each other along, rather than being "unequally yoked"—like an ox and a donkey—where they work against each other in a detrimental fashion. Descriptive, isn't it?

Do you remember the following passage from the dating chapter? The same principle applies to friendships.

> Do not be unequally yoked together with *unbelievers*. For what fellowship has righteousness with lawlessness? And what communion has light with darkness? And what accord has Christ with Belial? Or what part has a believer with an unbeliever? 2 Corinthians 6:14–15

But what about professing Christians who are "practicing" sin? Should they be your friends?

> I wrote to you in my epistle not to keep company with sexually immoral people. Yet I certainly did not mean with the sexually immoral people of this world, or with the covetous, or extortioners, or idolaters, since then you would need to go out of the world. But now I have written to you not to keep company with anyone named a brother, who is sexually immoral, or

covetous, or an idolater, or a reviler, or a drunkard, or an extortioner—not even to eat with such a person. 1 Corinthians 5:9–11

So what does this mean, practically, for you at college? Let me summarize: Possessors shouldn't date, marry, or enter into a close friendship or enterprise with an unbeliever or backslidden Christian. Why? Because the Possessor will invariably be pulled down spiritually.

While it may be hard to believe, certain "friends" (unbelievers or professing Christians) will *intentionally* try to pull you down, out of resentment for your having something they don't: faith in Christ, purity, joy. Don't be fooled by a smiling face; it can sometimes be a deceptive face. This type of person won't rest until they make you compromise.

> Do not enter the path of the wicked, and do not walk in the way of evil. . . . For they do not sleep unless they have done evil; and their sleep is taken away unless they make someone fall. Proverbs 4:14–16

For this reason, only fellow Possessors should make up your core group of close friends. "What?! How unloving! What about witnessing to others? What about all those Compromisers, Pretenders, and unbelievers—don't they need friends too?"

I am not saying to shun anyone, but rather to *regulate* non-Possessors to an *acquaintance* level of friendship or less, to a point where your interaction with these peers is lessened so that you won't be detrimentally affected. No friendship is worth compromising your integrity and testimony before God and others. At the same time you can maintain enough contact with them to be a witness for Christ.

Detrimental Friendships—Why?

One of the hardest questions to answer is why we get involved in detrimental friendships in the first place. It's certainly common and easy to do. Everyone, and I mean everyone, has an innate desire to be accepted and appreciated. Sometimes a Christian becomes involved with the wrong person, for the wrong reasons, to receive that acceptance or appreciation. She may want to be liked by the popular clique or the jocks or the pretty girls because she inwardly desires to be a part of that group.

Or sometimes a Christian becomes involved in detrimental friendships because he secretly craves the "fun" they're having—the parties and everything that goes along with it. He thinks to himself, "These guys are a lot more fun than my Christian friends." His flesh dictates with whom he spends his time.

Or sometimes a Christian becomes involved in a detrimental friendship because—are you ready for this?—Satan has purposely placed a stumbling block in the form of a "friend." Satan knows precisely what type of person appeals to us—looks, interests, intelligence, money, popularity—and presents the wrong person in our path to trip us up.

Or sometimes a Christian becomes involved in detrimental friendships because the people are simply nearby—classmates, dorm mates, teammates, workmates. In other words, because they're there! This is like meeting your new college roommate and immediately assuming that he or she is worthy of being your close friend just because you're going to live with each other. That is no criteria for a friendship. Will you be roommates? Yes. Acquaintances? Maybe. Close friends? Well, it depends.

Depends on what? What kind of person he or she is, of course!

Not being able to discern a person's character or the downright denial of the reality of someone's character leads to detrimental friendships. So how can you sharpen your discernment when it comes to friends?

It takes two things: plenty of time and careful consideration.

You are going to be encountering loads of new people when you arrive on campus. New faces will be everywhere—it's practically peer overload! You have no idea what anyone is like, where they come from, and what their values are. At first glance it can be difficult to tell the Overcomers from the Compromisers from the Pretenders from the unbelievers.

You know how it is—everyone seems like a "nice person." We don't tend to equate the people the Bible describes as "evil" or "fools" with people around us, especially not our friends. The difficulty is that people are very skilled at displaying a shiny exterior while concealing their sinful, unredeemed interior. Discerning someone's character takes wisdom.

This is not the case with God though. He sees right through people. He looks at their hearts.

> For the Lord does not see as man sees; for man looks at the
> outward appearance, but the Lord looks at the heart. 1 Samuel
> 16:7b

And that's what you need to do when it comes to potential friends—you need to look beyond their exteriors into their hearts.

Take Your Time

How do you do that? How can you find those mutually beneficial friends? First things first: *Take your time*. There's no rush. No one's going anywhere. You don't need five new friends by Friday.

Give yourself two months and a dozen experiences with any given person before going from introduction to acquaintance to friendship. Don't get too close too quickly. Even if you sense an instant kinship, take it slowly, as your first impression might be mistaken. Remember this: Mutually beneficial friends aren't made in a minute, they're made in a month (or two).

Careful Consideration

Now for the "careful consideration" part. What does that mean? It means you put your brain and spirit to work. It means you actively *choose* your friends based on their character rather than being chosen by others or settling for detrimental friendships. It means you're on the lookout for fellow Overcomers. It means you have a plan for picking your peers.

> The righteous should choose his friends carefully, for the way
> of the wicked leads them astray. Proverbs 12:26

Words?

First, listen to their words. What kind of words come out of the person's mouth? It doesn't settle the matter for someone to use Christian lingo or say, "I'm a Christian." As you know, any "Professor" can say that. On the other hand, if you hear profanity, like using the name of God or Jesus in vain, or four-letter obscenities, this is a telltale sign of that person's heart. Jesus said this:

> A good man out of the good treasure of his heart brings forth
> good; and an evil man out of the evil treasure of his heart brings

forth evil. For out of the abundance of the heart his mouth speaks. Luke 6:45

According to this verse, when someone uses foul language or talks fondly of sin, you're dealing with an "evil man" with a sinful heart. His mouth is uttering what is in his heart. This won't be a mutually beneficial friend. You will have to regulate this person as an acquaintance with whom you might share your faith down the road. This person is definitely not a candidate for your friendship at this point.

Actions?

Second, if their words are acceptable, the next test is to observe their actions. Does this person maintain sexual purity and sobriety? Is this person involved in sinful activities on a regular basis? Bottom line— does this person live like a follower of Jesus? If basic biblical principles are consistently being violated, this person is not a candidate for friendship. Regulate the friendship to an acquaintance level or less.

Association Principle

One last thing: Check out with whom this potential friend associates. You can tell a lot about a person by his or her friends (and foes). If they spend much of their time with other Possessors, that's a good sign. If not, be wary. As birds of a feather flock together, so true Christians will want to flock up with others like themselves.

There you have it—choosing friends is about *discerning their hearts.*

- Take your time.
- Listen to their words.
- Watch their actions.
- Note their other friends.

. . . And then make a wise decision.

The Friend Test

Before moving on to other ways you can successfully interact with your peers in college, let's use the above friendship discernment guidelines to put your current friends to the test. Which of your present friendships are beneficial, detrimental, properly regulated, or underutilized? Don't know? Never thought about it? Well, let's find out.

Write down the names of ten of your friends—your closest friends, good friends, companions, acquaintances—in a vertical column.

Now, on the left side of each person's name, quantify on a scale of one to four how much intentional personal interaction you have with that friend, either in person (e.g., meal, movie, activity, relaxing) or via phone or email.

Use the following general scale:

1: very little (once a month, acquaintance)
2: infrequently (few times a month, companion)
3: frequently (couple times a week, good friend)
4: very often (almost daily, very close friend)

Now, on the right side of each person's name, again on a scale of one to four, quantify that friend's level of Christian maturity using the friendship discernment guidelines in the above paragraphs (i.e., discerning their words, actions, associations).

Here's the scale:

1: unbeliever
2: professing Christian, but unclear if possessing Christian (Professor only)
3: clearly a genuine Christian (Possessor)
4: very strong Christian (Overcomer)

Ready to find out the results—which of your current friends are beneficial, detrimental, properly regulated, or underutilized?

Your Beneficial Friendships: Putting together the numbers before and after the person's name, your beneficial friendships will read 4–4, 4–3, 3–4, or 3–3. In other words, these are your close or good friends who are committed Christians with whom you interact often. These are friendships that pull you up spiritually and make you a stronger person.

Your Detrimental Friendships: Again, putting the numbers together before and after the person's name, your detrimental friendships (hope you don't have any!) will read 4–1, 4–2, 3–1, or 3–2. These are your close or good friends who are either unsaved or just professing Christians. If you continue to interact with these close friends as often as you do, you will be pulled down spiritually as sure as the day is long.

Your Properly Regulated Friendships: Your regulated friendships will read 1–1, 1–2, 2–1, or 2–2. These are unsaved or professing acquaintances or companions with whom you interact infrequently. Apparently, you've recognized that these friends will not strengthen you spiritually, and because of this, you've regulated down the amount of time and communication you have with them. Wise.

Your Underutilized Friendships: Your underutilized friendships will read 1–4, 2–4, 1–3, or 2–3. These are your committed Christian acquaintances or companions with whom you're not spending enough time. You are missing out on a beneficial friendship. You need to recognize these friends and regulate UP the amount of interaction you have with them.

Time Spent	Name	Christian Maturity	Type of Friendship
3	Sally	4	Beneficial
4	Joe	1	Detrimental

Now, of course, this "friend test" isn't perfect. There is an intangible dynamic to some of your friendships that only you can answer: Is there a personality problem with one of your strong Christian companions or acquaintances that keeps you from interacting more often?

Or are you spending lots of time with an unsaved or professing Christian friend because you are genuinely motivated to share your faith with him or her? Christians should have interaction with unbelievers and professing Christians, but careful consideration should be given to the following question: *Who is pulling whom which way?*

This friend test is simply designed to help you recognize the state of your current friendships by putting some of the peer discernment guidelines to practice. I'll bet you learned something about your present friendships that will help you choose wisely in college!

Christian Groups on Campus

Another way to successfully interact with your peers in college is to find and regularly attend a biblically sound Christian organization's events or meetings on campus during the week. Do not take your time on this! The very first week of school, seek out and then get plugged into a Christian campus group like Campus Crusade for Christ, Navigators, or Fellowship of Christian Athletes.

But the emphasis, once again, is on "biblically sound." Just like in your academic classes, you're going to have to use your newfound discernment skills to make sure the teaching is solidly scriptural. Campus Christian organizations are a great source to find those mutually beneficial friends—friendships that can last for a lifetime and that can help you be an Overcomer.

Church, Steeple, People!

And don't forget about church. The percentage of students who stop attending church skyrockets once they get to college. While it might not be convenient or you might feel like sleeping in like everyone else, it is vital for you to find and attend a Bible-teaching church every Sunday.

By the way, going to church isn't a suggestion—God *commands* that believers assemble regularly to worship Him. Being involved in a church gives you three for the price of one—you get quality interaction with God *and* your peers *and* your authorities (church leaders) and thus raise your spiritual GPA!

The bottom line is that every Christian needs fellowship with like-minded Christians on a regular basis. Start your week with church on Sunday, attend a Christian organization's meetings on campus midweek, and spend time with your Possessor friends in between. All these things will help to offset the conforming power of campus life from rubbing off on you.

The wrong approach to interacting with your peers is to be outnumbered by the wrong type of friends, believe you can be an island unto yourself, or think that your friends don't influence you. God never intended Christians to be loners—Possessors need like-minded fellowship to be Overcomers. Period.

> As iron sharpens iron, so a man sharpens the countenance of his friend. Proverbs 27:17

One caveat. There may, in fact, be times when you have to stand all alone for a while. The whole gang may be going one way—the wrong way—but your responsibility as a representative of Christ is to hold your ground or walk away. Sometimes you will feel as if you're being pulled in two different directions. My advice? *Give in to God pressure rather than peer pressure*. This may be hard, this could be lonely, but it's the right way. And you're really never alone:

> For [Jesus] Himself has said, "I will never leave you nor forsake you." Hebrews 13:5b

Interacting successfully with your peers takes guts—it often requires making hard decisions. You may have to break off a friendship that is having the wrong kind of influence on you. You literally may have to avoid that person. Your soul and your relationship to God are more important than any human friend.

Don't be deceived—friendships can often *feel* good but actually be detrimental to you spiritually. Being able to *recognize* the impact of a potential friendship and then *regulate* that relationship—closer or more distant—takes wisdom and willpower.

As you understand the power of peers and actively choose mutually beneficial friendships on campus, not only will you enjoy having great friends for a lifetime, but you will be well on your way to mastering the second fundamental of your college game plan for victory!

VERY IMPORTANT PRINCIPLE:

Interact with your peers successfully in college by choosing mutually beneficial friendships.

MESSAGE TO MEMORIZE:

He who walks with wise men will be wise, but the companion of fools will be destroyed. PROVERBS 13:20

PERSONAL COMMITMENT:

I will choose fellow Possessors as my friends in college and will regulate all others as acquaintances.

Signature:

Date:

GAME PLAN FUNDAMENTAL THREE:
INTERACTION WITH YOUR AUTHORITIES

Forget *positive* role models for a moment. Whoever said "You can learn a lot from *negative* examples" was on to something.

What do most students think as they head off to college?

"Whew—I'm finally on my own! No one around to tell me what to do. I can make all my own decisions. I will stay out as late as I want and do whatever I want. Yeah, I finally have my freedom."

Translation: "No more authority!"

They don't want Dad and Mom telling them what they can and cannot do and what time they have to be home. They don't want high school teachers telling them to do their work or to be to class on time. And they've had enough of their pastor or youth group leader telling them how to live.

They disregard this verse:

> Therefore humble yourselves under the mighty hand of God, that He may exalt you in due time, casting all your care upon Him, for He cares for you. 1 Peter 5:6–7

And hate this verse:

> Likewise you younger people, submit yourselves to your elders. Yes, all of you be submissive to one another, and be clothed with humility. 1 Peter 5:5a

These are negative examples and you can learn what *not* to do from them. Most incoming freshmen want full and complete "freedom," and they want it right now. And that is exactly what they get . . . along with the bondage to sin that this kind of uninhibited, unaccountable, and irresponsible freedom inevitably leads to. With far less authority present at college, it's no wonder a state of spiritual and moral anarchy exists on most campuses.

Professor Serpentine Is Back!

Even with their rebellious reputation, college students certainly didn't originate the concept of freedom from authority. Can you guess who did? You've met him before. Let me reintroduce the negative role model of all negative role models—Professor Serpentine.

Even with his highly exalted position of angelic prominence in heaven, Satan—or Lucifer, as he's called in this case—couldn't stand the idea of submitting to his *one* authority—God. So just like many college students, Lucifer rebelled against God. He was expelled from heaven for his rebellion. Here is the account:

> How you are fallen from heaven, O Lucifer, son of the morning! How you are cut down to the ground, you who weakened the nations! For you have said in your heart: "I will ascend into heaven, I will exalt my throne above the stars of God; I will also sit on the mount of the congregation on the farthest sides of the north; I will ascend above the heights of the clouds, I will be like the Most High." Yet you shall be brought down to Sheol, to the lowest depths of the Pit. Isaiah 14:12–15

Pride

Do you notice any similarities between the attitude of Lucifer and the attitude of many college students? The attitude is one of *pride*. It's all about "I" ("I" being in the center of "pride"). "I will be like the Most High" or "I will do what I want in college." "I am the master of my ship—no one's going to tell me what to do." "I know a better way; I don't need advice, counsel, or help." Pride says, "What pleases me?" while humility says, "What pleases God and others, including my authorities?"

Resenting or resisting authority is simply an external sign of a prideful heart. As mentioned earlier, pride is first on the list of the things God hates. He even goes so far as to resist the proud person.

> God resists the proud, but gives grace to the humble. James 4:6b

Humility

Contrast the prideful Lucifer and many college students to the One who perfectly interacted with His authorities—Jesus Christ. He was the Son of God, yet He humbled and submitted himself and obeyed His Father's will. Notice the benefit for doing so.

> And being found in appearance as a man, He humbled Himself

and became obedient to the point of death, even the death of the cross. Therefore God also has highly exalted Him and given Him the name which is above every name, that at the name of Jesus every knee should bow, of those in heaven, and of those on earth, and of those under the earth, and that every tongue should confess that Jesus Christ is Lord, to the glory of God the Father. Philippians 2:8–11

When we have an attitude of humility and properly submit to our authorities, we are imitating Jesus. On the other hand, when we have an anti-authority, I-centered attitude, we are imitating the father of rebels— Satan. Not only is he a liar, as we learned in the last chapter, but his pride won't allow him to submit to God.

The concept of submission is something our human nature naturally dislikes. God gave us the freedom to make our own choices, and we vehemently resist anyone getting in the way of that. But while it may go against your natural inclination, submission to authority, or as I like to put it, successful *interaction with authority* is the third and final fundamental of your game plan for victory on campus.

Four Types of Authorities

Let's get one thing straight: God has designed a human structure of authority to *help* us—*not* to spoil our fun. Through interaction with our various human authorities, God *directs* our ways, *protects* us from sin, and *teaches* us wisdom. He also tests our humility and faith through interaction with authority. God never intended you to be a one-person committee!

So who are the human authorities with whom you are to interact? The Bible specifies four distinct groups:

Parents: "My son, hear the instruction of your father, and do not forsake the law of your mother" (Proverbs 1:8).

An Overcomer friend of mine said this about his parents: "When I was in college, I decided never to do anything that I would be ashamed of if my parents were present." This defines honoring your parents.

The recurring theme of submission to parental authority is a thread that runs through the entire Bible. Honor your parents and you will be blessed; shun your parents and you will be cursed.

I know what you're thinking: "But you don't know *my* parents—

they're out of touch, they're really difficult, they don't understand!" Actually, I do know your parents. They're imperfect people that God uses to convey His will to you. Make every effort to hear, honor, and obey their counsel. When you're off at college, the game plan calls for you to interact with your parents often. Talk with them on the phone weekly and exchange email every few days. If you live close enough, make it a point to get home on a regular basis to reconnect and benefit from their influence. Believe me, this interaction is hugely important to your success on campus.

Civil leaders: "Let every soul be subject to the governing authorities. For there is no authority except from God, and the authorities that exist are appointed by God. Therefore whoever resists the authority resists the ordinance of God, and those who resist will bring judgment on themselves" (Romans 13:1–2).

Your federal, state, and local governmental authorities are pictured here—the president, governor, mayor, police. Think about what this passage says: God himself put them all in place to lead and keep order. Your responsibility? Obey your leaders and the law!

Church leaders: "Remember those who rule over you, who have spoken the word of God to you, whose faith follow, considering the outcome of their conduct" (Hebrews 13:7).

As college students lose or resist interaction with their parents and resent interaction with civil leaders, interaction with church leaders in college often goes away too. Why? Because a high percentage of college students stop attending church in college. Once again, prioritize being involved in a Bible-teaching church and seek interaction with the pastor, other church leaders, or even an older person or couple who can mentor your Christian walk.

Employers or teachers: "Bondservants, obey in all things your masters according to the flesh, not with eyeservice, as men-pleasers, but in sincerity of heart, fearing God" (Colossians 3:22).

When you are an employee, treat your employer with respect and heed his word. Do everything you can to make him or her be successful. Be the best employee you can be, not just for your own benefit but as a representative of Christ.

When you are a student, treat your elders (yes, your professors) with respect. Even the godless, anti-Christian ones I mentioned earlier.

They may have rebelled against the authority of God; don't you rebel against their authority, an authority God has set in place for you. Besides, for them to see their need for Christ, they may first need to see the humility of Christ in you.

The One Exception

"But," you say, "my parents and professors aren't Christians." "My boss at work is an evil dude." Don't underestimate God—He works equally well through your Christian and non-Christian authorities.

But there is one exception for interacting with your authorities: *You must never obey any authority that commands or advises you to do something contrary to God's Word.*

This is where you draw the line. If your parents tell you to lie on your college application about your community involvement, you should not do it. If a church leader advises you to not pay taxes to the government because your tax dollars will fund a bad government program, you must not heed him. If your professor shows pornography in class under the guise of "art," you must leave.

God and His Word must always stand before man and his word. God is always your highest authority. But any other command or counsel from your authorities that doesn't directly violate Scripture, you can know that God has allowed for your protection or direction. If you don't like it, respectfully petition for a different option.

The Labrador Lesson

Let me illustrate the final fundamental of your game plan by giving you a "lesson from my Lab." There I am standing in the driveway of my home with my yellow Labrador retriever at my side when a rabbit appears on the front lawn of the house *across* the street. My Lab sees the bunny and instantly moves to "greet" the rabbit on the other side of the road. What my dog does not see is the car speeding through the neighborhood.

Since I'm my dog's authority and I always look out for his well-being, I immediately tell him to come back to me. He now has a choice: He can disobey my authority, keep going toward the temptation, and suffer the consequences of getting hit by a car; or he can obey my authority (*even though he may not understand why*), come back to me, avoid getting hurt, and receive my praise and future trust.

This is how God works through your interaction with human authorities. He sees the big picture; we do not. He knows what is best for us; we often do not. Our responsibility is simply to obey now, trust Him, and (possibly) understand why later.

Successful interaction with your authorities is the final key to a high spiritual GPA. As you excel at this third fundamental of your game plan, you will discover that God protects you and directs your life through your authorities.

Rebels resist authority and suffer the consequences. Overcomers utilize their authorities and reap the benefits. They understand what it means to listen, heed, honor, obey, trust, and submit to their authorities—they know it's their path to victory and blessing.

VERY IMPORTANT PRINCIPLE:

God protects you and directs you through successful interaction with your human authorities.

MESSAGE TO MEMORIZE:

Remind them to be subject to rulers and authorities, to obey, to be ready for every good work. TITUS 3:1

PERSONAL COMMITMENT:

I will seek out and submit to my authorities in college— parents, church, government, employers/teachers.

Signature:

Date:

GAME PLAN ON A POSTCARD

Before I stepped out on the Centre Court of Wimbledon for the biggest match of my tennis career, my brother sat beside me in the locker room with a postcard in his hand. On it was the game plan for that match. To my complete surprise, the points on the postcard were not the complexities of the game of tennis, but rather the most basic fundamentals—"watch the ball, move your feet, be aggressive."

My brother understood the same thing I have been telling you—being able to execute the fundamentals under pressure is the key to success.

I have described the three most important fundamentals of your college game plan so you can have spiritual victory on campus: interaction with God, interaction with your peers, interaction with your authorities—your spiritual GPA. As you diligently work to improve at these fundamentals, you will be successful in college, and you will be an Overcomer.

But before we close this section, here is your own college game plan for you to copy (or cut out) and post on your wall:

— — — — — — — — — — — — — —

Daily: Interact with God through *reading the Word and praying*.

Weekly: Interact with God by *hearing a pastor's message on the radio or Internet*.

Bi-weekly: Interact with your authorities by *staying in touch with your parents*.

Midweek: Interact with your peers and authorities in a *campus Christian group*.

Sundays: Interact with God, your peers, and your authorities at *church*.

All week: Interact with your peers through *mutually beneficial friendships*.

— — — — — — — — — — — — — —

PERSONAL COMMITMENT:

I will focus on the fundamentals of my game plan in college—successful interaction with **G**od, my **P**eers, my **A**uthorities—so that I can be an Overcomer.

Signature:

Date:

11. DOWN BUT NOT OUT

"Get up, lad, get up!"

In the must-see Oscar-winning film *Chariots of Fire*, a famous running coach uttered these words after watching Eric Liddell, a Christian sprinter and the movie's main character, trip and fall to the track in the midst of a pre-Olympic race.

And "get up" Liddell did, coming from way behind to incredibly win the race. He may have been down, but he was definitely not out.

This scene is an excellent metaphor of your race in college. You now have the perfect game plan. But let's be frank, there is no way you will perfectly execute it. Yes, strive with all your heart to be like the perfect example, Jesus Christ, but as sure as you're reading these pages, there will be times when you will think, say, and do the wrong thing. In short, you will sin because you are human.

As you now well know, there are many pitfalls in college that can trip you up and make you stumble to the ground—the three Pillars of Peril being the major ones. Couple them with other traps like cheating, lying, or not doing what *should* be done in a given situation, and navigating through college completely unscathed becomes an impossible endeavor.

"Pobody's nerfect" is true . . . even for Possessors.

But Possessors have what it takes to be Overcomers, and that's just the point—they *overcome,* not only the obstacles but their own sinful failures, with the strength of the indwelling Holy Spirit. They may fall, but they quickly get up, change course, and continue on with the race.

Not so for all others like Compromisers and Pretenders. They fall harder and more frequently, stay down in their sin longer, don't learn from their mistakes, and often just give up on the race. Staying mired in sin becomes a bad habit that shapes their future.

This is exactly how "spiritual shipwreck" occurs in college: Every-one—Possessor, Compromiser, or Pretender—sustains cracks in his or her boat and takes on water, but only the Overcomer quickly and deci-sively gets rid of the water, fixes the hull, and sails on. The others take on water, do little or nothing, and get swamped.

Sometimes, though, that's how our human nature likes it. What's easier—lying on the track or getting back up to run the race? It's easier to fall than to run, easier to give in to the flesh and do little about it. It's much harder to strive, to compete, to expend effort to run the race and be victorious. But this is what Possessors do because they're running to please their Master, Jesus Christ, and not their own desires.

> Therefore we [*Possessors*] also, since we are surrounded by so great a cloud of witnesses [e.g., past Christians, Jesus], let us lay aside every weight, and the sin which so easily ensnares us, and let us run with endurance the race that is set before us, looking unto Jesus, the author and finisher of our faith, who for the joy that was set before Him endured the cross, despising the shame, and has sat down at the right hand of the throne of God. Hebrews 12:1–2

There is a great reminder in this passage for Possessors—something Christian college students need to remember: Remember who, from the heavens above, is watching you run the race in college. Remember to stay on your feet and not get tripped up by sin. Remember for whom you are running and how Jesus endured to the end in His own race.

It is a reminder of the first of four Cs describing an Overcomer.

OVERCOMERS COMPETE!

Yes, compete in the college race like your life depends on it (and it does). Understand that college is a spiritual battle against Satan and your flesh, and valiantly fight against being bogged down by sin. Strive to remain on your feet. Do everything you can to not fall. Know that the less you fall into sin, the more you can stay on your feet and keep running on course.

Compete to be *holy,* for this is God's will for you.

> But as He who called you is holy, you also be holy in all your conduct, because it is written, "Be holy, for I am holy." 1 Peter 1:15–16
>
> Do you not know that those who run in a race all run, but one receives the prize? Run in such a way that you may obtain it. And everyone who *competes* for the prize is temperate [self-restrained] *in all things.* 1 Corinthians 9:24–25a

The Pleasure Principle for Possessors

Now, you might think that, with all this talk about avoiding the Pillars of Peril, improving your spiritual GPA, and competing for holiness, college isn't going to be any "fun." Well, if your definition of fun must include sinning against God, you need to immediately abandon this flawed perspective. If you don't, I promise you that you'll find out the hard way that the temporary pleasures of your sinful "fun" are not worth the enduring consequences.

I have a better idea for your having fun in college, and you might be surprised by what it is. Are you ready for this? I call it the Pleasure Principle for Possessors.

Do whatever you want . . . without sinning in the process.

How can I say that? Because if you truly love God more than anything or anyone else (including yourself), you can do whatever you want because what you want will be what God wants!

Want to go out late with your friends? By all means go ahead, but don't get drunk or break the law in the process. Want to go on a co-ed dorm trip for the weekend? Pack your bags, but keep yourself morally pure. Interested in meeting a particular guy or girl? Go for it, but be sure to keep the "Dating Game" chapter in mind. Go ahead—have lots of fun in college; just avoid sinning in the process.

The wisest man who ever lived, King Solomon, put it this way:

> Rejoice, O young man, in your youth, and let your heart

cheer you in the days of your youth; walk in the ways of your heart, and in the sight of your eyes; but know that for all these God will bring you into judgment. Therefore remove sorrow from your heart, and put away evil from your flesh, for childhood and youth are vanity. Ecclesiastes 11:9–10

Translation: Do what your heart desires, but know that God will judge your every thought, word, and deed—whether good or evil. This is what it means to have a "fear of the Lord"—you are reverently aware that God is constantly watching you and that you will have to give an account to Him someday for every thought, word, and action. That should be enough to make you compete for holiness!

For the eyes of the Lord run to and fro throughout the whole earth, to show Himself strong on behalf of those whose heart is loyal to Him. 2 Chronicles 16:9a

Now, when I say, "Do whatever you want," I am *not* saying to put yourself in tempting situations where you're likely to get burned or even in circumstances where there is an appearance of evil. I am saying to imitate the Overcomer, who competes to be holy and at the same time is ready to withstand or flee when sinful scenarios arise.

A prudent man foresees evil and hides himself, but the simple pass on and are punished. Proverbs 22:3

Sin is a cruel master—the more you sin, the stronger its grip becomes. The complete "freedom" in which college students indulge actually brings them into bondage—they cannot *not* sin!

Competing for holiness reduces the frequency and necessity of the next three Cs. That's why it's important to do everything possible to stay on course. True, it takes effort to swim against the collegiate stream, it takes strength to resist popular culture, it takes wisdom to keep from falling. But when you compete for holiness and succeed, it only makes you stronger and less likely to fall the next time around.

But even the best competitors lose once in a while. Even Overcomers stumble and fall at times. What do they do next? How do they respond?

OVERCOMERS CONFESS!

You lied to your friend, you cheated on a test, you went too far with your girlfriend, you drank too much, you used profanity or obscenity, you grumbled to God, you slandered a classmate, you told off your mother—*you sinned and you're lying on the track!*

Now what? Well, as long as you're down on your knees, confess your sin to God right then and there! Don't wait. Don't minimize it. Don't rationalize it. Human beings have the amazing capacity to rationalize any sin. And I mean *any* sin. Hitler believed he was providing a service to the world with his death camps.

What does confessing your sin mean? It means you "agree with" God that you have broken His perfect standard. It means you want to restore broken fellowship with Him. It means you acknowledge that you were wrong and He is right. It means you accept full personal responsibility for what you have done. It means you come to God with a broken spirit because you have disobeyed Him.

> The sacrifices of God are a broken spirit, a broken and a contrite heart—these, O God, You will not despise. Psalm 51:17

It also means you ask the forgiveness of any person you have directly offended by your sin: "I was wrong for doing this or saying that—will you forgive me?" Not "I'm sorry *if* you were offended," but rather "I was wrong and I'm sorry for hurting or offending you." The person may not forgive you, but you are still right to ask for his or her forgiveness.

When we sin, the indwelling Holy Spirit convicts our conscience that we have done wrong, that we're guilty of offending God. Think of your conscience as being similar to your nervous system telling you to immediately take your hand off a hot stove. If you ignore the warning, you'll further burn yourself, causing even greater injury.

Just like sensitive nerves in your hands, a sensitive conscience protects you from further sinful injury—that is, unless you dull or sear your conscience by repeatedly ignoring it. This is why people can sin and have no remorse toward God or others—they have suppressed their conscience over and over again and have been told to ignore their guilt. Once again, this is a Lie:

> If we say that we have no sin, we deceive ourselves, and the

truth is not in us. 1 John 1:8

Overcomers listen to their convicting consciences and immediately confess their sin to God. They don't wait a week. They don't try to weasel around it. They don't allow themselves to indulge further in the sin. They want to get back on their feet right away.

They also don't create legalistic boundaries that are *more narrow* than God's. They check the conviction of the Spirit to make sure it's consistent with the Word of God. They don't get bogged down by false guilt.

Yes, Overcomers fall, but they quickly act to restore their relationship with God by confessing their sin. They obey *and* believe the following verse:

> If we confess our sins, He is faithful and just to forgive us our sins and to cleanse us from all unrighteousness. 1 John 1:9

And then they're back on their feet . . . a little wiser and a little more wary. They don't want to do *that* again! What happens next? The third C, of course.

OVERCOMERS CHANGE!

Figure out what caused you to sin, and make a change of course to avoid it the next time. Did you put yourself too close to a tempting situation? Were you spending time with detrimental friends? Has your Christian walk slackened because you haven't been interacting with God?

Whatever led to your fall, make a decision to change. This is what it means to repent: You change your mind (thoughts) about your sin— realize how offensive to God your sin really is—which in turn changes your future behavior (actions). Your thoughts become your actions, right? Changed thoughts bring changed actions.

Unbelievers can't, won't, or don't change. They continually make the same mistakes; they commit the same sins over and over. Even professing Christians sometimes do the same. They epitomize the following proverb:

> As a dog returns to his own vomit, so a fool repeats his folly. Proverbs 26:11

Because unbelievers don't have the indwelling Holy Spirit, they're impotent to change. But as we discussed in an earlier chapter, the very same Spirit that powerfully resurrected Jesus Christ from the dead and gave Him victory over sin is the same Spirit that indwells every Possessor. You have the power to change because of this identification with your Savior and Lord. You have the potential to be victorious over sin.

Reading and understanding chapters 6 and 8 in the book of Romans is key to applying this truth. Just a sample:

> Likewise you also, reckon yourselves to be dead indeed to sin, but alive to God in Christ Jesus our Lord. Romans 6:11
> For the law of the Spirit of life in Christ Jesus has made me free from the law of sin and death. Romans 8:2

Yes, you can change and have victory over sin, but it isn't easy. It requires following through on *hard* decisions such as breaking off a detrimental dating relationship, avoiding certain places, guarding your eyes and ears, and silencing wrong impulses. Change is always hard, but the good news is that God will give you the grace (power) to change and stay on course!

To slightly alter the slogan of a popular retailer, "You can do it . . . the *Spirit* will help."

OVERCOMERS CONTINUE!

You competed for holiness. Unfortunately, you still took a tumble. You quickly confessed your sin and got back to your feet. You changed course to avoid repeating it.

Now, *continue* running the race!

It's easy to beat yourself up over sin so that you can't move forward: "How could I have done such a thing? God could never forgive me for what I did." We punish ourselves in the present for what we did in the past. We spend time brooding over past failures with wouldas, couldas, and shouldas.

Forgive yourself because God already has.

It's easy to carry around past failures, which serve only to limit you from reaching your future potential. "I'll never be anything now" or "God can't use me because of what happened in the past." We haul around this burden of sin baggage and never let it go.

Forget your sin because God does.

Yes, God forgives and forgets your sin, and now He wants you to continue forward and sin no more.

> As far as the east is from the west, so far has He removed our transgressions from us. Psalm 103:12
> And Jesus said to [the woman caught in adultery], "Neither do I condemn you; go and sin no more." John 8:11

Even the apostle Paul, who previously *murdered* Christians, said this about his past and continuing the race:

> Brethren, I do not count myself to have apprehended; but one thing I do, *forgetting those things which are behind and reaching forward to those things which are ahead,* I press toward the goal for the prize of the upward call of God in Christ Jesus. Philippians 3:13–14

When you became a Possessor, God forgave every one of your sins—past, present, and future. Therefore, you don't have to *ask* for forgiveness when you sin; rather, confess your sin and *claim* the forgiveness He has already given you at the point of your salvation. For the Christian, this is about restoring broken fellowship with Him.

Now, of course the other tendency is to *minimize* our sin. "So I sinned again. No big deal—God loves me and forgives me." But sin *is* a big deal to God. One of your sins alone would have been enough to nail Jesus to the cross. Just one sin by you would justifiably send you to hell. We should never take advantage of or presume upon God's grace and forgiveness.

> What shall we say then? Shall we continue in sin that grace may abound? Certainly not! How shall we who died to sin live any longer in it? Romans 6:1–2

Let's say you were fifty million dollars in debt, and no matter what you did in life, you could never pay it off. Every dollar you would ever earn would go directly to your creditor. This is not a bright future for you. As a matter of fact, it's downright hopeless.

Then all of a sudden someone comes forward and pays off the fifty million dollars, completely relieving you of your debt. But not only that, the person agrees to pay any future debt you incur. Unbelievable!

How would you react? You would be ecstatic! You would be so thankful. You would do anything to please that person. You would be extra careful not to incur any more debt. You would *continue* on with a spring in your step!

This is precisely what Jesus Christ did for you when He died on the cross for your sin. He paid in full the debt you owed to God for your past, present, and future sin. What you could never pay off, He paid in full for you.

Do you think He wants you to brood over your sin debt further so it limits your progress? Of course not. He wants you to continue forward with thankfulness, loyalty, and holiness.

Jesus overcame the power of sin on the cross. Now He wants you to be an Overcomer too! Continue running the race.

$)—\bullet—($

You will fall down at times in college, but if you're a Possessor, you are definitely not out. A Possessor has what it takes to overcome, not just the obstacles on campus, like the three Pillars of Peril, but to overcome his own sinful failures too. That is what makes a Possessor an Overcomer.

Overcomers *compete* with all their might to be holy so they can avoid sinning in the first place. They aren't *sinless*, but they do *sin less* because they know it's easier to complete the race if they don't fall frequently or severely.

Yet when they do stumble and fall, Overcomers immediately and humbly *confess* their sin to restore fellowship with God. They agree with God and accept full responsibility for their sin.

Overcomers *change* their minds about their sin and repent. They learn from their mistakes, purpose to chart a new course, and take the necessary steps to stay on track.

And finally, Overcomers *continue* running the race because they know God has forgiven and forgotten their sin. They don't carry with them what God has cast away.

Possessors certainly aren't immune to tripping up on the college track, but with the Spirit of an Overcomer, they get right back in the race to surge victoriously across the finish line!

VERY IMPORTANT PRINCIPLE:

Compete for holiness in college. Confess your sin when you fall. Change your course when you get up. Continue running the race.

MESSAGE TO MEMORIZE:

Do you not know that those who run in a race all run, but one receives the prize? Run in such a way that you may obtain it. And everyone who competes for the prize is temperate in all things. Now they do it to obtain a perishable crown, but we for an imperishable crown. Therefore I run thus: not with uncertainty. Thus I fight: not as one who beats the air. But I discipline my body and bring it into subjection, lest, when I have preached to others, I myself should become disqualified. 1 CORINTHIANS 9:24–27

12. CHOOSING A COLLEGE—
SAINT OR STATE?

Or maybe the Marines?

High school is history—*now* what do you do? "Go to college this fall, of course," you say. Not so fast.

Do you have the money to pay for college? If so, is a Christian or a secular college better suited to you? One near home or three states away? How are your grades? What do you want to study in college? What type of career are you targeting?

Most important, *why are you even going to college?* To learn stuff? To have fun? Because it's the thing to do?

Just as a reminder, there is no law stating you have to go to college three months after completing high school. High school graduates have plenty of options—attending college being just one of them. As a matter of fact, for many professing Christian high school graduates, attending college—any college—directly after high school would be the *unwise* thing to do. They would be walking right into their University of Destruction.

The assumption that every Christian high school graduate is prepared mentally and spiritually for college is like saying all bananas ripen at the same time. Check out the banana section at your local grocery store sometime. Only certain bunches—the bright yellow ones—are ready to eat. The green ones still have some maturing to do. They're not any worse but are just at a different stage of maturity.

It is the same with Christian teens. The ripe ones are mature spiritually and focused academically. They know why they're going to college and are prepared spiritually for the experience. In short, they know their purpose and are on a mission.

On the other hand, many Christian teenagers are like the green, unripe bananas. They are immature spiritually, not grounded in their faith, and have little or no purpose in college. "The Pillars of Peril— What?" "Academic interests? Um . . ." They go off to college because it seems like the next step, when in fact they're ill prepared for the obstacles—*and opportunities*—on campus.

And then there's always the *sink or swim* philosophy: Even if you're not ready for college, spiritually or academically, go anyway and either survive or shipwreck. "I'll learn in time" or "I guess I'll just have to figure some things out the hard way" is the mantra. Not a good idea. Would anyone leave port on an unseaworthy boat knowing there was a significant probability of shipwreck? Of course not! The consequences of *spiritual* shipwreck in college are far too serious and enduring to leave home without being fully prepared. Sadly, in some cases recovery and restoration never come. It's always wiser to set sail with a sturdy ship that can withstand the storms.

Back to the important question: Why are you going to college?

Let me offer a two-fold objective—the first spiritual and the second academic.

Spiritual Objective

First, your *spiritual* objective. God's goal for you in college is not only to survive the Pillars of Peril but to *thrive* spiritually on campus. He desires for you to be the best possible representative of Jesus Christ. He wants you to become more like Him so that you can be "salt and light" on campus, a "fragrance of Christ" to the lost and to the saved. People sense when you're a Possessor—it's as if you're walking around campus with a T-shirt that says "Jesus Team Member." Representing Christ is your spiritual calling—and responsibility—in college.

For we are to God the fragrance of Christ among those who

are being saved and among those who are perishing. To the one we are the aroma of death leading to death, and to the other the aroma of life leading to life. 2 Corinthians 2:15–16

Academic Objective

Second, your *academic* objective in college is to prepare yourself for a future career. For example, if you want to be a medical doctor, you'll need to specialize in sciences like biology and chemistry. If you want to be an engineer, you'll need to specialize in math. If you want to be a teacher, you'll need to specialize in English, history, science, composition, etc. If you want to be a pastor, you'll need to specialize in Bible, theology, and pastoral ministry.

In other words, college isn't *primarily* about broadening your *general knowledge base*. Sure, using the first couple years of college to discover your interests and take useful core courses like English and writing is very profitable. But choosing irrelevant classes as you cruise aimlessly through college is not only a waste of time but a waste of money. The ideal scenario is to identify your general interests as early as possible, take specific classes to hone those interests into a major, and then work in a similar field after college. That's called maximizing your college experience.

Know *why* you're going to college! The Possessor should have a spiritual and an academic objective—a purpose. The goal spiritually is to grow stronger in your faith and become more like Jesus Christ, and the goal academically is to prepare yourself for your future career.

SPIRITUAL GPA TEST

So how do you know if you're ready for college spiritually and academically? Why not take a personal inventory? Examine yourself today. Let's evaluate your spiritual GPA and your level of academic purpose by answering the following questions on a scale of zero to four:

0. Never
1. Seldom
2. Sometimes
3. Frequently
4. Always

Interaction With God

Score:

_____ Do you interact with God regularly through reading His Word and praying?

_____ Are you involved in a church, a worship service, and/or a Christian group weekly?

_____ Do you have a desire to grow in your faith by other means, such as being mentored, reading Christian literature, or listening to a sound Bible teacher on the radio or Internet?

_____ Add the scores and divide by 3. This is your **Interaction With God Score**

Interaction With Your Peers

Score:

_____ Are your friends mutually beneficial and properly regulated?

_____ Do you prefer being with other Christians?

_____ Can you stand alone, even withstanding embarrassment or ridicule?

_____ Add the scores and divide by 3. This is your **Interaction With Your Peers Score**

Interaction With Your Authorities

Score:

_____ Do you hear and heed the advice of your parents, your church leaders, your teachers, your employer, and the police?

_____ Do you see your authorities as useful for protection and direction?

_____ Do you plan on seeking out and honoring your authorities in college?

_____ Add the scores and divide by 3. This is your **Interaction With Your Authorities Score**

_____ Now average your three scores. What is your **Spiritual GPA**?

If you scored three or four, you are *spiritually* ready to take on the challenge of college. If you scored two or lower, you are in danger of a University of Instruction turning into your University of Destruction. If you are between two and three, you need to increase your spiritual GPA to give yourself a better chance of victory on campus.

ACADEMIC PURPOSE TEST

Now what about your academic purpose? Using the same scale you used for your spiritual GPA test, answer the following questions:

Score:

_____ Are you interested in discovering and honing your academic interests in college?

_____ Are you looking forward to the educational opportunities in college to prepare you for a future career?

_____ Are you committed to getting the best possible grades in college?

_____ Now average these scores to find your **Academic Purpose Score.**

Once again, if you score three or four, you are *academically focused* and ready for the opportunity college affords to prepare you for a future career. If you score two or lower, you need some "ripening" and should look at some other options for this fall (we'll cover those in a minute). If you are between two and three, well, it's a judgment call.

Were you honest with yourself? Would someone who knows you well—your mom or dad, your best friend, your youth group leader—rate you the same way? Why not ask them?

With a decision this momentous, it is the perfect situation to take to them. Show them the test above and ask them to grade you. Or sit down and have a talk with them. The decision to go to college, let alone *which* college, is truly one of the most important decisions you will make in life. Getting counsel from those who know you best and care most about you is indispensable . . . and biblical.

Without counsel, plans go awry, but in the multitude of counselors they are established. Proverbs 15:22

If there's a mismatch between your own personal assessment and your counselors' assessment, find out why and don't proceed with any decision until a consensus can be reached. But if your own personal assessment matches your counselors', you can be confident in any decision you make about college. This is precisely how to utilize your authorities!

OPTIONS FOR EIGHTEEN-YEAR-OLDS

All right, let's move on to your post–high school options. Everyone likes options, right? You certainly have plenty of them! Let's list your post-graduation options in multiple-choice fashion:

A. Home/Work
B. Military
C. Christian College
D. Secular College
E. All of the Above
F. None of the Above

A. Home/Work

"What?! Live at home, work, and not go to college immediately? How could you suggest such a thing? I'll get way behind all my friends!"

As we've been discussing, some high school graduates are not ready spiritually or academically (or financially) to go to college three months after high school. So stay home and work for a year!

If you have a low spiritual GPA, you're setting yourself up for destruction if you attend college before you're ready. If you don't have serious academic intent, you're just wasting your time and money. For one year (maybe two), why not discover a potential career path and at the same time raise your spiritual GPA in the safer environs of home? Besides, home cooking beats dorm food every time.

Home

While your friends are battling the Pillars of Peril in college, you can live at home and greatly minimize the danger of getting mired in sin and being negatively influenced by godless professors. Instead of being distracted by the college scene, you'll have quality time to interact with God. Instead of a uniform-age peer environment, you'll interact with known friends in different age groups. Instead of very little authority present, you'll have familiar faces like your parents and church leaders around to help. And you can sleep in your own bed.

As you read earlier in this book, the transition from home life to campus life is huge. Taking that factor out of the equation gives you some extra time to raise your spiritual GPA. Now, let me say that someday you're going to have to stand on your own two feet in the real world, but for many high school graduates, there's certainly nothing wrong with delaying it a year or two.

Work

The "real world" means having a job, making a living, paying your bills, and supporting a family. So why not get a taste of the real world and at the same time find something you really enjoy? The sayings go, "If you love your job, you never have to work another day in your life," or "Find something you love to do and figure out a way to make a living at it." Use your home/work year to discover your *passion* in life.

Ask yourself, "If I could have any job in the world, what would it be?" A wilderness guide? A prosecuting attorney? A skateboard designer? A television news anchor? A hair stylist? A detective? The point is to find a purpose that makes you passionate!

Whatever your "dream job," go work, apprentice, volunteer, or shadow in that field. Find their place of business and inquire about doing something—anything—within that line of work. Believe me—you'll learn a lot more *experiencing* the career than *theorizing* about it in college.

Don't like it after a few months? Move on to another line of work that interests you. You're just trying to find out what you like, what fits you, and whether you would want to pursue that career in the future. Of course, you won't get your dream job right away, but you'll get a flavor for the field and know whether you want to further study it in college.

The home/work option is a great one for those who need to raise their spiritual GPA or for those who need to discover their academic/career passion in life. Reevaluate or retake the spiritual GPA and academic purpose tests after your home/work year—college may then be right for you if you're spiritually ready and academically focused. If the truth be told, you'll probably be light-years ahead of your peers. What a difference a year can make!

B. Military

"Uncle Sam wants you!" Maybe you should want him too. For those of you who decide to wait on college for a couple of years, serving in the military may be the option for you. Let's compare the military with college:

- In the military you'll learn about loving and serving your country and others. In college some professors preach a hatred of America, and most students serve just themselves.
- In the military you'll learn discipline, a most important trait in life. In college most students don't even understand the word.
- In the military you'll learn the importance of authority. In college most students resent and rebel against authority.
- In the military you'll learn about personal responsibility. In college most students are shirking theirs.
- In the military you can travel the world and learn valuable skills. In college most students' travel consists of going from their dorm room to the classroom.

As if this isn't enough, the government will pay for your college after you fulfill your service. How's that for a deal?

As with any of the post–high school graduate options, there are some downsides and dangers to serving in the armed forces (not the least of which is combat). The peer culture can be difficult in the military, and certainly some aspects of the Pillars of Peril will be present. But serving in a branch of the military might be the right choice for you before college. Like the home/work option, you'll have another few years of "ripening" before heading off to college. And who knows, you might become commander in chief someday!

C. Christian College

So you have a high spiritual GPA and good academic purpose. You're ready to take the plunge and enter college immediately after high school. You want to further your education in an environment with Christian students and faculty. "I'm going to a Christian college!" you declare. Wonderful, but choose with care.

Christian colleges can be *fantastic* for you. Christian colleges can be *terrible* for you. Say what?

Attend a biblical Christian college and you'll benefit immensely from an education with a Christian worldview. Attend a liberal Christian college (biblically errant due to humanistic theology) and you might become more confused and disillusioned about your faith than ever.

Attend a biblical Christian college and you'll have professors who strengthen your faith. Attend a liberal Christian college and you'll have professors questioning the inerrancy, the sufficiency, the relevancy, the inspiration, the truthfulness of the Bible.

Attend a biblical Christian college and you'll most likely experience a conducive environment for spiritual growth with better peer influence and less Pillar pressure. Attend a liberal Christian college and, well, you might be better off at State U, where you can clearly discern the difference!

Remember, just because it's "Christian" doesn't mean it's *really* Christian. Like recognizing the huge difference between a professing Christian and a possessing Christian, you need to find a *possessing* Christian college—one where the Word of God is the absolute, final authority, one where the Holy Spirit indwells the majority of students and faculty.

Read the mission and doctrinal statements of the school, visit the campus, get references and recommendations, and talk to the faculty. Do they believe Scripture is inspired by God, the universe was created by God, Jesus Christ is the Son of God, the miracles in the Bible are literal, and salvation comes by faith in Christ alone?

And finally, remember that a Christian college is not representative of the real world, where Christians are the minority. The transition from Christian college to the secular working world can be traumatic after college. Also, spiritual apathy can be contagious at Christian colleges if students don't want to be there. Downsides notwithstanding, for many Christian students, a biblical Christian college is *heaven on campus!*

D. Secular College

The next option is a secular or nonreligious college. You have plenty of options within this option—state universities, private universities, community, technical, trade, or junior colleges. The general rule of thumb, I've found, is the more elite the university (e.g., Ivy League, Stanford), the more godless it will be. Community and technical colleges tend to play things more "straight up." In other words, the "smarter" they are, the more "foolish" they are.

> For you see your calling, brethren, that not many wise according to the flesh, not many mighty, not many noble, are called. But God has chosen the foolish things of the world to put to shame the wise, and God has chosen the weak things of the world to put to shame the things which are mighty; and the base things of the world and the things which are despised God has chosen, and the things which are not, to bring to nothing the things that are, that no flesh should glory in His presence. 1 Corinthians 1:26–29

Must be that pride thing again. This is not to say that elite private universities should be avoided and that state, community, or technical colleges are always the better choice. The Possessor with a high spiritual GPA can be an Overcomer *anywhere*. Yet the allure of an elite university—even with a full scholarship—with its promise of career and financial benefits is certainly not worth compromising your Christian character if you're not spiritually prepared.

> For what will it profit a man if he gains the whole world, and loses his own soul? Mark 8:36

Nowhere are the Pillars of Peril more menacing than at secular colleges. While their impact varies from campus to campus, you should be ready for strong sexual temptation, pervasive abuse of alcohol, and anti-Christian, humanistic philosophies being taught openly by professors. This is the world and all it has to offer.

Which can be a good thing for certain Christians, I might add. Some see this environment as a mission field and an opportunity to sharpen their own faith. They prefer good and evil standing out in distinct contrast to one another. After all, as resistance makes the weight lifter stronger, so does the testing of your faith . . . if you purpose to be an Overcomer.

If you want to lessen the negative impact of a secular college, live at home (or off campus with other Possessors), stay away from the radical anti-Christian professors, and be especially careful of the "soft sciences"—philosophy, psychology, humanities, sociology. Doing this will give you some relief from the daily humanistic brainwash. But even more important, you need to focus on the fundamentals of your game plan—interaction with God, your peers, your authorities—to make it through with your faith intact.

E. All of the Above
F. None of the Above

Don't forget about the last two options. Perhaps "all of the above" is for you. Do home/work for a year, serve in the military for a couple years, attend a Christian college afterward, and then finish your degree at a secular college. This is a rare (and long!) route, but an option nonetheless, right?

Or perhaps just as unique is "none of the above." Maybe college or the military is not for you. You know what you want to do with your life, have enough education to pursue it, and want to get going with your career. Hey, it takes all types to make the world go round. Careers that don't require *higher* education are definitely not *lower* in God's eyes.

>—•—<

So what will it be—home/work, military, saint, state, or no college at all? Choosing your post–high school graduation option takes careful consideration. Defaulting to college three months after high school isn't always the best decision, spiritually or academically. Every person matures at a different pace, and an accurate self-assessment, with the help of your authorities, is vital to choosing your right path.

Go to college only if you know your spiritual and academic objectives—spiritually, you are there to represent Jesus Christ and become more like Him; academically, you are there to discover and prepare for a future career.

If your spiritual GPA needs work and your academic focus is lacking, by all means choose the home/work or military option. If you do go to college, living at home can be an extremely helpful buffer from the Pillars of Peril. And by the way, these aren't "lesser" options; rather, they're "different strokes for different folks."

In reality, your greatest threat is *not* staying away from college for a year or two but that a University of Instruction will turn into your

University of Destruction. This is what you want to avoid at all costs!

Choosing your post–high school option is all about matchups. Match yourself up to the option that best suits you.

- Going to an elite secular college if you have a low spiritual GPA is a bad matchup.
- Choosing the home/work option if you have a high spiritual GPA and high academic purpose is a bad matchup.
- Serving in the military if you have a high spiritual GPA but unclear academic purpose is a good matchup.
- Choosing a biblical Christian college if you have a good spiritual GPA and solid academic purpose is always a good matchup.

Remember—it's not the *institution,* it's the *individual.* Overcomers will overcome anywhere. Compromisers and Pretenders will fall even in the "safest" environments. Know thyself—let your spiritual GPA and your level of academic purpose dictate your post–high school decision.

To slightly alter a tennis expression: "Game, set . . . *matchup!*"

VERY IMPORTANT PRINCIPLE:

Match your spiritual GPA and your level of academic purpose with the post–high school option that suits you best.

MESSAGE TO MEMORIZE:

A man's heart plans his way, but the Lord directs his steps.
PROVERBS 16:9

CONCLUSION

SHIPWRECKED . . . THEN SAVED!

And now you'll know the rest of the story.

After two months at Stanford, I was spiritually shipwrecked—a University of Instruction had turned into my University of Destruction. I was a statistic, one of the many professing Christian students who "lose their faith" in college. Thinking back, it is not in the least bit surprising.

Did I understand how difficult the transition would be to college? No, I didn't give it much thought.

Did I consider my own vulnerability and lack of preparation? No, I thought I was a Christian and could handle the experience just fine.

Did I purpose to be an Overcomer in college? No, I entered college a Compromiser and "rode the fence" while there.

Did I realize the strong allure and life-changing danger of the three Pillars of Peril? Not really. I was more enticed by the temporary "fun" the first two Pillars offered rather than considering the enduring consequences.

Did I know the important difference between a *professing* Christian and a *possessing* Christian and know which one I was? No, I thought a Christian was a Christian. After all, I grew up in a Christian home, made a profession of faith at age five, went to church with my family, and kept a Bible in my dorm room.

Did I make a commitment to and maintain moral purity? No.

Did I date only Christians and not play the *dating game*? No.

Did I stay away from alcohol? No. Did I stay away from drugs? Yes. (Alas, a victory!)

Did I avoid the negative influence of sensual, worldly music? No, I listened to what I liked and to what felt good.

Did I recognize the humanistic lies of godless professors and replace them with the truth of the Bible? Not really (but I would've actually had to *attend* class more frequently to do that!).

Did I have a game plan and diligently work on improving my spiritual GPA—my interaction with God, Peers, and Authorities? No, I hardly read the Bible, had plenty of detrimental friendships, and resisted my authorities.

Did I pursue holiness so I wouldn't fall, repent of my sin when I did, and change course so as to not repeat my mistakes? No, I habitually sinned and found ways to rationalize it.

Did I choose a college that matched my spiritual GPA and academic purpose? No, an elite secular college far from home was not a good matchup with my low spiritual GPA and level of academic purpose.

>—•—<

That is certainly a lot of no's, especially for a young man coming from an "idyllic" Christian background. One would think things should have been different. I could have been a shining light for Christ on a secular campus using the platform awarded me as the "Most Outstanding Freshmen Athlete" at Stanford. But I didn't—I pleased myself, not God.

Instead of being an Overcomer, I fed my flesh and it *overcame* me. Even in the midst of spiritual shipwreck, though, I still had this inner voice whispering to me about my sinful course. Because of my Christian upbringing, I knew my life wasn't right before God, but I felt powerless to change. I had good intentions at times, but I would willingly and discouragingly fall back into sin.

Though they tried, my parents weren't able to help either. Of course, they were only seeing the tiny tip of the iceberg. If they had known the entire story of my spiritually destructive path, they would have insisted on a plane ride home for me. But I was very skilled at hiding my sin and deceiving others. I may have been fooling a lot of people (including myself), but I certainly wasn't fooling God. He was watching the whole time.

Despite my inner conflict, I continued to be outwardly successful. My grades, although not as good as in high school, were acceptable even with little study and low academic purpose. I excelled on the tennis court, helping Stanford win the national tennis championship in the spring. I had the typical popularity of a top athlete on campus.

And then my freshmen year ended at Stanford. I had become what the Bible calls "a double-minded man, unstable in all his ways" (James 1:8). I was being pulled in two different directions: My flesh yearned to be fed, while that inner voice—my ever-diminishing conscience—knew better. There was a battle inside of me, and my flesh almost always won.

But now I had a decision to make. Should I go back to Stanford in the fall for my sophomore year or turn professional in tennis? Still a top prospect for the pro tour, I was offered significant endorsement contracts from clothing and racket manufacturers. And although winning the collegiate national team championship was a thrill, it didn't seem worth a year's wait for another crack at the team or individual title.

In the back of my mind, though, was that little voice warning me that college was going to further destroy my soul if I returned to the same course. Not college itself, per se, but my spiritual inability to overcome the battle would take me farther down the wrong road.

I made my decision—I chose the home/work option and turned professional. Only I wasn't really home much and my career path was already chosen, so my life consisted of traveling around the world ten months a year, earning a living as a professional tennis player.

Instead of relief, though, the tennis tour brought a new set of problems. A change of scenery didn't change my heart, of course. Sure, the collegiate Pillars of Peril were behind, but a new tempting triad further fueled my double-mindedness. They were *fame, fortune, and success.* They are the post-collegiate Pillars of Peril that working men and women face. They deceive career-minded professionals into thinking happiness comes from achieving any or all of them, yet when attained, they offer only emptiness and a desire for "just a little more."

But achieve them I did . . . and quickly. At age twenty-two, just three years after turning professional, I was known across the world (fame), was a millionaire (fortune), and was ranked number twelve in the world after reaching the semifinals of Wimbledon (success).

Summing it all up was the license plate on my Jeep: "LOVE2B1"

I still wasn't happy or content.

As if that wasn't enough fame, fortune, and success, I won the largest prize money tournament in the *history* of tennis—the Grand Slam

Cup—in Munich, Germany, later that year. As I stood there holding aloft the trophy in front of fourteen thousand fans, my life was about to take a small but significant turn. Within ten minutes of winning the greatest title of my career, I watched as the fans streamed out of the stadium and the grounds staff folded chairs and removed banners—it was over in a flash. I remember the distinct thought that my greatest moment of triumph was extremely short-lived. For the first time in my life, I realized the temporary "high" of fame, fortune, and success couldn't deliver lasting fulfillment.

I had just tasted some truth, but I didn't swallow it. I continued along my same course of outward success and inner conflict. My relationship with my parents was badly strained; I was involved in another detrimental dating situation; I yearned to make more money and appear in television commercials. I was living the typical self-centered existence of a pro athlete. Sure enough, what had started in college had only continued years later in a different form.

But that little voice kept speaking to me. I knew, *just knew*, I was on the wrong road, but I couldn't seem to get off it. But then two years later, at age twenty-four, everything was about to change . . . for the better.

My parents asked, no, *persuaded* me to attend a Christian seminar that featured some basic principles from the Bible. A hardened case by this time (I had seen and heard all this Christian stuff before), I reluctantly listened to the seven biblical principles presented in the seminar:

1. Clear Conscience
2. Meditation on Scripture
3. Submission to Authority
4. Moral Purity
5. Forgiveness
6. Yielding Rights
7. Self-Acceptance

By the end of the seminar, I was in complete shock. Not the "good Christian boy" I thought I was, I had actually broken *every single one of those principles!*

- I had a guilty conscience before God and others.
- I didn't read the Bible, let alone meditate on it.

- I rebelled against my authorities.
- I was morally impure.
- I held bitterness toward others without forgiving them.
- I angrily confused privileges for my rights.
- I misunderstood God's design for my life.

I came to the rightful conclusion: *I am not a true Christian.*

This was revolutionary for me. Me, a sinner? Me, offending God? Me, as bad as anyone else? Me, deserving of hell? Yes, yes, yes, and yes. For the first time in my life, I saw myself as God saw me. I saw my need for forgiveness, my need to be right with God, my *need* to get on "the narrow way that leads to life."

I was bent, but not completely broken . . . yet. A decade of sinful momentum held me in its grip for several more months until I decided to stay home from my annual trip to the Australian Open. I just couldn't take another step with the immense burden on my back. The inner voice was screaming now, not whispering.

For at least an hour a day for the next two months, I sat home reading and studying the Bible. I completed study guides, I memorized Scripture, I prayed to God, and I made commitments to read the Word and be morally pure. It was heart-wrenching, emotionally draining, and even tear-jerking. I never had an appetite for any of this before, but miraculously a desire had sprung up within me, and I ran with it.

But most important during this time, I repented of my sin and put my faith in Jesus Christ as my Savior and my Lord. I humbled myself before God and confessed my years of sin against Him and others. I purposed to change my course and asked for His strength to do so. I believed Jesus Christ had died on the cross for my sin, and I committed to being His follower. I was spiritually born. *I became a "born-again" Christian.*

This definitely wasn't about becoming more "religious"—going to church, praying more often, being baptized, receiving communion, getting confirmed, reaffirming my Christian heritage, volunteering my time, turning over a new leaf, or doing any good works to justify myself before God. This was about getting down on my knees and saying, "God, have mercy on me, a sinner." This was a *supernatural* transformation of my heart.

And a transformation from Professor to Possessor.

Surprisingly and encouragingly, I *immediately* began to have victory over my sinful thoughts, actions, and motives. The temptation to return to my old self came fast and furious, but the now-indwelling Holy Spirit was there to remind me of God's Word and give me the power to overcome. It certainly wasn't easy—I had to end one relationship, restore others, and "take every thought captive" that entered my mind to keep on course. I obeyed even when I didn't understand why. I kept telling myself, "Just put one more day between your new life and your old life, *just one more day.*" God gave me one victory after another. For the first time in my life, I was an Overcomer!

I was thrilled. Now my desire to please God and to not offend Him was greater than my desire to please myself and sin. The Spirit strengthened, my flesh weakened. I memorized significant passages of Scripture that dealt directly with my greatest points of weakness. Just as the Bible promises, it was my key to continuing victory.

The Bible was right: "God resists the proud but gives grace to the humble" (James 4:6b). God had resisted me all those years because of my self-enthroned existence, but when I humbled myself, He gave me the grace—the power to do His will.

Sure, it took plenty of time to learn and renew my mind to a whole new way of life. This was done every day as I interacted with God through Bible study and prayer, as I interacted beneficially with like-minded peers, as I submitted to my God-ordained authorities.

My spiritual GPA soared! I didn't become sinless, although I did *sin less*—I no longer habitually practiced sin. The important thing was that I was on that narrow road . . . and lovin' it!

Perhaps the greatest part of it all was being able to put my head on my pillow at night knowing I was in a right relationship with the God of this universe. I was *never* able to do that previously. That simple pleasure is worth far more than the temporary pleasures of the Pillars of Peril or all the fame, fortune, and success the world can ever offer. Yes, I finally had peace and joy and hope and could truly say, "Life without Christ is a hopeless end; life with Christ is an endless hope!" (Anonymous).

Warning and Wisdom

We're on the homestretch—let's finish strong! At its most basic level, this book offers you two things: a *warning* and *wisdom*.

Warning . . .

The warning stems from the fact that college is an extremely dangerous time for *all* young people, Christians included. As if the transition from home life to campus life isn't difficult enough, the three Pillars of Peril stand poised to entrap and destroy countless souls. They destroy through temptations of the *body* (sex, drugs, alcohol) and temptations of the *mind* (secular humanism or religious humanism taught by the professors).

In the grand scheme of the universe, the battle you will face on campus represents the broader war between God and Satan: Satan has been condemned to spend eternity in hell, and in the meantime, he's trying to take as many souls down with him as possible. His motive certainly matches his nickname—*Destroyer.*

I can't think of a more conducive environment that exists on earth for Satan to work his destruction. Young people are more vulnerable and impressionable than at any other time in their lives as they make their big transition to college. They are encouraged to "experiment" sexually, party hearty, and "open their minds" to the godless philosophies and errant theologies of man.

Satan has many ways to divert you from following "the way, the truth, and the life"—Jesus Christ. His philosophy is "whatever works." Whether it's sexual sin, drug and alcohol abuse, or deceptive philosophies of the professors, like evolution, moral relativism, or false religion, Satan just wants to lead you away from the one Way that will send you to heaven. And he doesn't care how long it takes.

Fortunately for him, there are many souls who follow willingly, often unknowingly, down his path. His devices feel, sound, and appear so attractive—if they weren't, no one would take the bait! Most college students eagerly swallow his lures, not realizing the present, future, and eternal consequences. There truly is "a way that seems right to a man, but its end is the way of death" (Proverbs 14:12).

With willing subjects in a willing environment, college must seem like shooting fish in a barrel for him—truly, Universities of Destruction.

Now, it would be nice (but naïve) to think the 50 percent of Christian students who say they have lost their faith in college will become followers of Christ later in life. My hunch is that most of them weren't genuine Christians in the first place and college only serves to lead them further astray.

The other 50 percent of Christian students who make it through college with their faith intact are Possessors—possessors of a genuine faith and the indwelling Holy Spirit. They may fall for a time, but they always get back on track. Once a Possessor always a Possessor, with all the necessary resources to be an Overcomer.

Taking the "I'm only young once" approach or the "I'll get back with God later" philosophy or the "I'll learn by experience" route is truly playing with fire—the fire in hell. Not only are the unavoidable consequences of sin bad enough, but not one of us knows the exact day of our earthly departure, when we will stand alone before God in judgment for our every thought, action, and motive. God is not fooled, is not mocked, and does not wink at "sowing your wild oats."

> Do not be deceived, God is not mocked; for whatever a man sows, that he will also reap. For he who sows to his flesh will of the flesh reap corruption, but he who sows to the Spirit will of the Spirit reap everlasting life. Galatians 6:7–8

The warning is loud and clear—your soul is at stake in college.

. . . *Wisdom*

I have a confession to make: Not one scrap of advice written in this book originated in my own mind. I plagiarized it all from another book—the Bible.

In the Bible God provides more than enough *wisdom* for you to overcome Satan and his collegiate schemes. It is not the wisdom of the world propagated in college by professors that relies on limited human intelligence, but the wisdom of the Word that reflects the infinite, perfect, powerful, and holy mind of God!

The wisdom to overcome stems from trusting in the Bible as your final authority and source for truth, and then applying it practically to the trials and temptations you will face on campus.

As if the Word of God isn't enough, you also have the example of One who embodied and used the wisdom of the Word as He overcame His *World of Destruction*. Jesus Christ is your perfect example of an Overcomer.

These things I have spoken to you, that in Me you may have peace. In the world you will have tribulation; but be of good cheer, I have overcome the world. John 16:33

But there is one ultra-important prerequisite for victory in college: To apply the wisdom of the Word and be an Overcomer on campus, you must first possess the Spirit that made Jesus Christ an Overcomer, the exact same Spirit that gave Him victory over temptation to sin and victory over physical death on the cross.

Without the indwelling Holy Spirit, you are powerless to overcome in college. With the indwelling Holy Spirit, you have all the power you'll ever need to overcome as you obey His leading.

How do you become a *possessor* of a genuine faith in Jesus Christ, a possessor of the indwelling Holy Spirit? You agree with God that you are alienated from Him because of your sin. You ask His forgiveness and purpose to change your course. You believe that Jesus Christ is the Son of God and that He came to earth to die on the cross in your place for your sin. You commit to making Him the Master of your life.

In return God gives you forgiveness of your sins, eternal life with Him in heaven, and the Holy Spirit to be your guide, helper, and comforter along the way. He even increases that important inner couplet—a love for Him and a fear of Him—so that your desire to obey Him is greater than your susceptibility to offend Him.

Yes, once you are a Possessor, *then* you can be an Overcomer.

And once you commit yourself to being an Overcomer on campus, it's just a matter of raising your spiritual GPA by excelling at the fundamentals of your game plan—interacting with **G**od, your **P**eers, and your **A**uthorities.

You successfully *interact with God* by spending time with Him *every day* through reading, studying, memorizing His Word, and praying. This renews your mind and helps you recognize and replace the brainwash of humanistic professors. This helps you recall and recite specific passages of Scripture when you are tempted to sin.

You successfully *interact with your peers* by discerning and choosing mutually beneficial friendships rather than ones that are detrimental to you spiritually and morally. This helps you avoid "unequally yoked" dating relationships that eventually compromise your faith.

You successfully *interact with your authorities*—especially your parents and church or Christian campus group leaders—by keeping in frequent contact with them and utilizing them for protection and direction while on campus. This points you toward God's will in your life and shields you from being on your own.

These are your resources for overcoming the Pillars of Peril. This is taking the wisdom of the Word and applying it practically to every situation you will face on campus.

And even more, the wisdom is also there to give you the right course of action when you fall. Possessors are occasionally *overcome* by sin, but they quickly get up (confess their sin), change course (repent), and continue running the race (persevere), determined once again to be an Overcomer.

Wisdom is also there to help you have a wonderful time in college yet to do so without sinning. For too many students life in college is defined by sin and a regression to immaturity. They have believed the lie that fun cannot be had without sin. Instead of going from boy to man and girl to woman, they go from boy or girl to fool.

Lastly, it's helpful to have godly wisdom as you make your decision on where to go to college. Matching up your spiritual GPA and your level of academic purpose to a Christian or secular college—or even the home/work or military option—takes wisdom that comes from the Word.

You have it all—a *warning* about college and the *wisdom* to overcome. You have heard the truth—not my truth, but God's truth.

So now, for most of you, you're on your way to college. What's it going to be—a University of Instruction or your University of Destruction?

In *Pilgrim's Progress*, one of the greatest books ever written, a Christian walking on the road of life from the "City of Destruction" to the "Celestial City" said the following:

> The hill, though high, I covet to ascend,
> The difficulty will not me offend,
> For I perceive the way to life lies here.
> Come, pluck up heart, let's neither faint nor fear,
> Better, though difficult, the right way to go,
> Than wrong, though easy, where the end is woe.

For those of you who resist or reject the message of this book, my hope and prayer is that your end would not be "woe" but rather that this book would continually be that little voice urging you to get off the broad way that leads to destruction and onto the narrow way that leads to life.

On the other hand, for those of you who *read* and *heed* the message of this book, you will surely conquer the "hill" of college and be able to triumphantly say, like the apostle Paul:

I have fought the good fight, I have finished the race, I have kept the faith. Finally, there is laid up for me the crown of righteousness, which the Lord, the righteous Judge, will give to me on that Day, and not to me only but also to all who have loved His appearing. 2 Timothy 4:7–8

To which I can only add, *Well done, Overcomer!*

APPENDIX

As a Ph.D. student at UCLA in the late 1980s, Gary Railsback studied approximately four thousand students who had answered either, "Yes, I am a born-again Christian," or "No, I am not a born-again Christian," on an incoming and outgoing collegiate survey administered by the Higher Education Research Institute (HERI) at UCLA.

The results were astounding: Depending on the type of college attended, as many as 51 percent of students who claimed to be "born-again Christians" as freshmen said they were no longer born-again Christians four years later. Just as surprising, there was little difference in the "faith attrition rate" whether students attended a religious or secular college.

Now, in 2005, Dr. Railsback, a professor at George Fox University, received from HERI the most recent survey data of students who answered, "Yes, I am a born-again Christian" upon entering college but then four years later answered, "No, I am not a born-again Christian." In the table on the next page, you can see that in almost every instance the results are even more disturbing.

References:

Higher Education Research Institute. "College Student Survey." Cooperative Institutional Research Program. *http://www.gseis.ucla.edu/heri/css_po.html*.

Railsback, G. L. "An Exploratory Study of the Religiosity and Related Outcomes Among College Students." Ph.D. diss., UCLA, 1994. *http://academic.georgefox.edu/grailsba/uclastudy.pdf*.

Author note: A special thanks to Dr. Gary Railsback for providing his original study and the updated data.

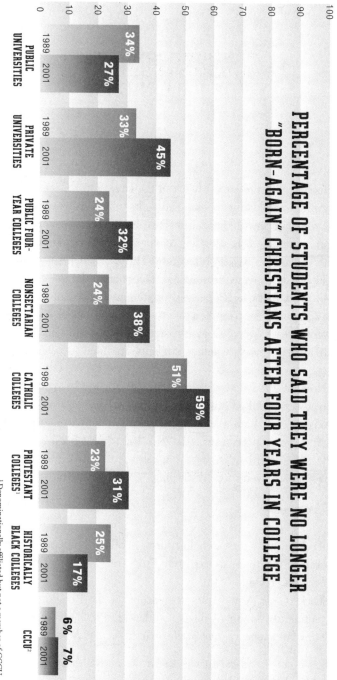

PERCENTAGE OF STUDENTS WHO SAID THEY WERE NO LONGER "BORN-AGAIN" CHRISTIANS AFTER FOUR YEARS IN COLLEGE

PUBLIC UNIVERSITIES
1989: 34%
2001: 27%

PRIVATE UNIVERSITIES
1989: 33%
2001: 45%

PUBLIC FOUR-YEAR COLLEGES
1989: 24%
2001: 32%

NONSECTARIAN COLLEGES
1989: 24%
2001: 38%

CATHOLIC COLLEGES
1989: 51%
2001: 59%

PROTESTANT COLLEGES[1]
1989: 23%
2001: 31%

HISTORICALLY BLACK COLLEGES
1989: 25%
2001: 17%

CCCU[2]
1989: 6%
2001: 7%

[1] Denominationally affiliated but not a member of CCCU
[2] Council for Christian Colleges and Universities

ACKNOWLEDGMENTS

For we brought nothing into this world,
and it is certain we can carry nothing out.
1 TIMOTHY 6:7

It is also "certain" that, in between, I owe everything to God, family, friends, and many others.

To Dad and Mom: Thank you for all you are and all you have done. I'm blessed and honored to be your son.

To Marnie: Thanks for teaming up on the title!

To Mark, John, and Brodie: Thank you for your insightful editing and input.

To Kyle, Natasha, and the Bethany House team: Thank you for believing . . . and delivering.

And to my Heavenly Father:

How can I say thanks for the things You have done for me—
things so undeserved, yet you give to prove your love for me?
The voices of a million angels could not express my gratitude—
all that I am and ever hope to be, I owe it all to Thee.
                              —Andrae Crouch, "My Tribute"

All right, Ben, I'll take you for a walk now. . . .